Ratan Tata

Neha Chander's professional journey began in the fast-paced world of journalism, took a short-lived detour through the advertising industry and finally found its footing in the dynamic field of publishing. This Delhi-born, Chhattisgarh-transplanted writer and editor has since wielded her editorial pen on everything – from travel guides to academic journals. When not chasing Oxford commas or exasperatedly correcting the use of apostrophes, she can be found in her small rural hideout, cataloguing birds and critters on iNaturalist, watching horror movies to relax, and debating extraterrestrial existence (jury's still out on the UFOs) with her four-legged therapy group – four cats, three dogs – all while her farmer spouse tends to his goat companions. Neha's interests range from historic events and famous personalities to human psychology and modern pop culture, accompanied by an eclectic playlist spanning Muse, Kendrick Lamar, Chappell Roan and everything in between.

RATAN TATA

A True Titan of Indian Industry

Neha Chander

First published in 2025 by Hachette India
(Registered name: Hachette Book Publishing India Pvt.Ltd)
An Hachette UK company
www.hachetteindia.com

All chapters have been researched and written by Neha Chander.

ISBN 978-93-5731-850-1

Hachette Book Publishing India Pvt. Ltd
4th/5th Floors, Corporate Centre,
Plot No. 94, Sector 44, Gurugram 122003, India

Typeset in Cambria 10.5/13 by Avishek Bhattacharya

by Manipal Technologies Limited, Manipal

Contents

Image Copyright Information

p. 21:	Harvard Business School: AevanStock/Shutterstock.com
p. 23:	Lakme: Everything You Need/Shutterstock.com
p. 24:	Tata Sierra: Karunesh Johri/Shutterstock.com; Jamsetji Nusserwanji Tata: Unknown Publisher/CCA-SA 4.0 International; Dorabji Tata: Unknown author/Public domain, US; Naval Tata: Prashantk2/CCA-SA 4.0 International
p. 24:	Tatanagar: Sanket_Mishra/Shutterstock.com
p. 31:	Tata Chemicals: Tata Chemicals Winnington Plant by David P Howard
p. 35:	Ratan Tata at MLSM College: Sungodnika/Shutterstock.com
p. 39:	Ratan Tata at the AeroIndia Airshow in Bengaluru: Aerospace Trek/Shutterstock.com
p. 40:	Tribal conclave: bijitdutta.com/Shutterstock.com
p. 41:	J.R.D. Tata: http://photodivision.gov.in/IntroPhotodetails.asp?thisPage=953
p. 46:	Tata Sierra: Karunesh Johri/Shutterstock.com
p. 48:	Tata Indica: C C Lathish/ Shutterstock.com
p. 51:	Vistara: Hardik Dedhia/Shutterstock.com
p. 54:	Bell Canada: Elena Berd/Shutterstock.com
p. 63:	TCS: PradeepGaurs /Shutterstock.com
p. 70:	Tetley Tea: Zety Akhzar/Shutterstock.com
p. 79:	Tata Steel plant in Wales: Chris Goddard/Shutterstock.com
p. 81:	Jaguar: Viikramaditya Rai/Shutterstock.com
p. 82:	Land Rover: PradeepGaurs/Shutterstock.com
p. 84:	Tata Nano: Thampapon/Shutterstock.com
p. 97:	Tata Memorial Hospital in Rajarhat, Kolkata: Indrajit Das/CCA-SA 4.0 International
p. 144:	Cyrus Mistry: Government Open Data License - India (GODL)

Preface

This book introduces a new strand to the **Quick and Concise (QC) series** with the first of our **biographies**. As is the signature of the QC series, the biography of **Ratan Tata** is full of information that enhances one's knowledge. And since the subject of this book is one of the foremost luminaries in business, the information also teaches one to dream big – inspires. Ratan Tata's illustrious career was not restricted to successes within India alone but was marked with some of the most talked-about global takeovers – Corus, Jaguar, Land Rover.

Contemporary India's most celebrated industrialist's life journey demonstrates not only how to adapt to changes but also how to bring about positive change, how to meet challenges – including failures. And what entrepreneurialism means in a world that shrinks with technological advancement every day. The book is not an unadulterated hagiography; it includes the controversial moments from Tata's life in an unbiased narrative. His life is a telling example of how to deal with ups and downs – the Tata Indica venture being a case in point.

His life also illustrates the key belief that has underscored the Tata legacy – business is not just about making money, it is also about being responsible, adventurous and generous. This is an essential lesson Ratan Tata's life aims to instil in everyone. His life and initiatives, inspired by a family legacy that he inherited, stand out as supreme examples of philanthropy and humility. He showed us how big businesses can give back to society, that too in an unassuming way.

This Quick and Concise no-frills biography is loaded with accurate and essential facts and interspersed with trivia and snippets that complete the picture. There are interesting note boxes, quotes, key numbers and pictures that enhance the narrative, making it clear, simple, light and fast paced even while describing the most serious moments of the industrialist's life.

CHAPTER I

EARLY LIFE AND BACKGROUND

- Introduction to the Tata Legacy
- Ratan Tata's Family and Heritage
- Education and Formative Years

Introduction to the Tata Legacy

Ratan Naval Tata, born on 28 December 1937, was a distinguished Indian industrialist and philanthropist whose groundbreaking influence extends far beyond the boardroom of the Tata Group and can be seen in the modern business and industrial landscape of India. This legendary scion of one of India's most revered business families passed away at the age of eighty-six on 9 October 2024, leaving behind a legacy of both innovation and social responsibility in the business sector. Widely admired for his humility and compassion, Ratan Naval Tata consistently prioritized ethical leadership and philanthropy and was known for donating a significant portion of his wealth to various charitable causes. As a result, his vision redefined corporate governance in India while also setting a high benchmark for future business leaders.

Ratan Tata remains a monumental figure in the history of India's economic and industrial evolution. His tenure as chairman of Tata Sons from 1991 to 2012 marked a golden period for the Tata Group, propelling its status from an Indian conglomerate to a formidable global entity. Under his stewardship, the Tata Group underwent significant diversification and expansion, as well as landmark acquisitions, including those of Tetley Tea, Jaguar Land Rover and Corus Steel. These efforts enhanced the group's global presence and modernized Indian industry. Ratan Tata's leadership also happened to coincide with a period of economic liberalization in India, during which he adeptly navigated these unforeseen changes.

Ratan Tata famously believed that businesses should play an active role in addressing societal challenges. This philosophy manifested through his countless initiatives in education, healthcare and rural development through the Tata Trusts. His approach to philanthropy was not just about financial contributions to various causes; it also harboured a deep understanding of community needs and sustainable practices. By allocating approximately 65 per cent of the group's profits to charitable projects, he ensured that the fruits of his success were shared with the less fortunate.

Ratan Tata's humility and approachability set him apart from many contemporaries in the corporate world. Despite presiding over one of India's largest conglomerates, he famously remained grounded and focused on fostering genuine connections with employees and stakeholders alike. This personal touch resonated deeply within his organization and contributed to the evolution of a corporate culture that values integrity and respect.

Perhaps one of the most significant aspects of Ratan Tata's legacy was his commitment to sustainability. Under his leadership, the Tata Group adopted a comprehensive sustainability agenda that was aimed at mitigating the Group's environmental impact. These measures were formalized through the establishment of the Tata Sustainability Group, which consolidated various initiatives for promoting sustainable practices across all Tata companies. In India, the group has been at the forefront of renewable energy investments, particularly through Tata Power – a leader in solar and wind energy projects in the country. Moreover, Ratan Tata advocated for clean technology and electric vehicles and championed the entry of Tata Motors into the electric vehicle market.

In addition to corporate sustainability, Ratan Tata has been instrumental in promoting organic farming and sustainable agriculture through the Tata Trusts. In recognition of the importance of food security and environmental health, his initiatives helped numerous smallholder farmers to adopt organic farming practices that focus on enhancing soil health, reducing dependency on chemical fertilizers and empowering and improving the livelihoods of local communities through training and provision of resources. With a deep interest in environmental conservation, Ratan Tata also fostered projects involving afforestation, water conservation and habitat restoration.

Ratan Tata's life work exemplifies the potential for business to be a force of good in society – something that could assist future leaders looking to navigate the complex global challenges emerging today.

The Tata Dynasty and Legacy

In the late eighth century, a small band of Zoroastrians set sail from their homeland in Persia, propelled by the winds of persecution that swept through their once-magnificent empire. As Islamic forces advanced, these refugees left their homeland behind to seek sanctuary across the seas, eventually landing on the shores of Gujarat, in a place known as Sanjan. Here, they encountered the Hindu ruler King Jadi Rana, who was initially hesitant to grant them permission to settle. To express his concern about the potential strain on local resources, he presented them with a full glass of milk as an emblematic gesture, indicating that his kingdom was already full.

In response, a wise Zoroastrian priest stirred a spoonful of sugar into the milk without spilling a drop, symbolizing their intent to blend harmoniously into the local community. This act greatly impressed the king, who granted them asylum under certain conditions – they were to adopt the local language and customs and relinquish their weapons. Thus began the remarkable advent of Parsis in India.

Over time, the Zoroastrians assimilated into Indian society while retaining their distinct cultural identity. They became known as ‘Parsis’, which means ‘people from Persia’, and established themselves as integral members of their new country. Their contributions to trade and industry were significant, with many Parsis transforming from agriculturalists to successful merchants and entrepreneurs. After their arrival, the port town of Surat became a bustling hub for the community, who seized opportunities in commerce that had previously eluded them.

Among the towns that became a home for this community is Navsari in Gujarat. This ancient town served as a refuge for many Parsis, as well as the place of origin of notable figures like Dadabhai Naoroji, India's first member of the British Parliament. It was here in Navsari that one Parsi family emerged over the decades as particularly influential – the Tatas.

The Tata dynasty as it is known today traces its roots back to the patriarch **Nusserwanji Tata**, who chose to venture into business rather than remain confined to the traditional priestly roles defined by his birth. Nusserwanji Tata belonged to a class of Zoroastrians known as *dasturs*, who had served the Parsi community as priests for generations. However, he was discontent with being destined to uphold religious tradition and recognized the changing tides of society and economy. So, Nusserwanji ventured into business in a bold move, leaving behind the familiar confines of Navsari and setting foot in Bombay (now Mumbai) to look for greater opportunities in business and banking.

In Bombay, Nusserwanji began to carve out a new path for his family. He envisioned a future where his son Jamsetji could thrive in a commercial environment with a high potential for success. Hence, he brought Jamsetji from Navsari to Bombay to immerse him in the new world of business.

Born on 3 March 1839 in Navsari, **Jamsetji Tata** joined his father in Bombay at the age of fourteen. His education at Elphinstone College ignited a lifelong passion for literature and learning, culminating in his graduation as a 'green scholar' in 1858. Although initially attracted to the world of academia, Jamsetji later became drawn to the world of commerce. In 1859, he was dispatched to Hong Kong by his father with the responsibility of expanding the family firm, thus marking his first foray into international business.

In December 1864, aged just twenty-five, Jamsetji Tata travelled to England to manage cotton consignments for his father's firm. During his four years in England, he immersed himself in learning the cotton trade and studying the operations of mills in Lancashire and Manchester. His entrepreneurial journey began in 1868 with the establishment of a personal trading firm, using a modest capital of ₹21,000. This venture proved fruitful as he secured contracts to supply military equipment abroad, generating significant profits that pushed him to explore the textile industry. In 1869, he partnered with his friends to purchase a dilapidated oil mill in Bombay, revitalizing it into the Alexandra Cotton Mill, which was sold profitably just two years later.

In 1874, Jamsetji set his sights on Nagpur, where he founded the Central Indian Spinning, Weaving and Manufacturing Company. His decision to establish this mill away from Bombay's textile hub was strategic – his goal was to capitalize on the local cotton production, as well as the railway access in the area. The Empress Mill, inaugurated in 1877, became a model of innovation and employee welfare with the introduction of advanced American machinery and labour protections.

In 1886, Jamsetji began a highly appreciated pension fund for his workers, followed by an accident compensation scheme in 1895, thus setting unprecedented standards for employee benefits that surpassed those of his Indian competitors. He also took on the challenge of reviving the struggling Dharamsi Mills, which he later renamed Svadeshi Mills, in 1886. This mill, aligned with the Swadeshi movement and primarily supported by Indian shareholders, faced significant hurdles, including plummeting share prices and a lack of dividends for two years. Determined to protect the Tata name that had become threatened by the mill's instability, Jamsetji used his personal funds to inject capital into the mill; this resulted in the mill's transformation into a high-grade textile producer, with the fabric produced here finding markets in China, Korea, Japan and the Middle East.

While in England, Jamsetji had attended a lecture by the philosopher Thomas Carlyle that inspired him to initiate an iron and steel industry in India. Despite the challenges posed by the British government's reluctance to support large-scale Indian enterprises, he remained resolute in his vision. He ultimately collaborated with British and American surveyors, including the notable Charles Page Perin, to identify iron deposits across India. Furthermore, his commitment to this venture led him to travel extensively for technical guidance on steel production.

The Taj Mahal Palace in Mumbai, the 'diamond by the sea', stands as an enduring symbol of Indian hospitality and architectural grandeur. Opened on 16 December 1903 by Jamsetji Tata with an investment exceeding £300,000, the hotel was conceived as a response to the racial discrimination he faced at Watson's Hotel of Bombay, which only admitted Europeans. Jamsetji Tata envisioned a hotel that would rival the best in the world. His goal was to create a world-class hospitality establishment that showcased India's potential. Designed in the Indo-Saracenic style, the Taj Mahal Palace was built with meticulous attention to detail and boasted luxurious furnishings sourced from Europe and beyond. The hotel featured electric lights, fans and even a power laundry – modern conveniences that were rare in Indian hotels of the time. It was equipped with four electric passenger lifts and had its own power plant, which ensured a continuous electricity supply. Additionally, the Taj offered unique services, such as a chemist's shop, a resident doctor and a Turkish bath, all designed to provide guests with unparalleled comfort and luxury. It quickly became a preferred venue for both dignitaries and celebrities. Over the years, the hotel has witnessed significant historical events, including its use as a military hospital during World War I as well as the devastating terrorist attacks of 2008. Today, it remains a defining landmark of Mumbai, renowned for its rich heritage and commitment to excellence in service.

After investing substantial resources in his pet project, Jamsetji passed away in Germany in 1904 before his dream could be realized. However, he entrusted his vision to his sons, Dorabji and Ratanji Tata, as well as his cousin R.D. Tata.

Jamsetji Tata was not only a pioneering industrialist but also a dedicated philanthropist. In 1892, he established the J.N. Tata Trust, which aimed to support higher education by sending deserving students to study abroad. This initiative benefitted many of India's early engineers, surgeons and barristers. In 1898, he donated his properties and funds to establish the Indian Institute of Science, a dream realized posthumously in 1911 with the institute's founding in Bangalore (Bengaluru now). Furthermore, with an interest in labour welfare, he introduced innovative practices, such as shorter working hours and improved working conditions, long before they became standard.

Prominent Members of the Tata Family

Jamsetji Tata's elder son, **Sir Dorabji Tata**, was born on 27 August 1859. After receiving his education at Gonville and Caius College, Cambridge, and St. Xavier's College in Bombay, Dorabji initially worked as a journalist at the *Bombay Gazette* before joining the family business in 1884. His leadership qualities and vision were instrumental in realizing his father's dreams, particularly the establishment of Tata Steel in 1907 and Tata Power in 1911.

Under his stewardship, the Tata Group expanded significantly, diversifying from its initial textile focus to include hydroelectric power, cement production and insurance. Sir Dorabji's commitment to sports also shone through as he championed the Olympic movement in India by financing Indian athletes for the 1920 and 1924 Olympics and serving as the first president of the Indian Olympic Association.

On 14 February 1898, Sir Dorabji Tata married **Lady Meherbai**, who was a remarkable personality in her own right, known for her advocacy of women's rights and education in India. She was the daughter of Dr H.J. Bhabha, a respected educational reformer in Mysore (Mysuru). Dorabji Tata first met Meherbai through his father, who had befriended the Bhabha family during his visits to Mysore. Their courtship blossomed over time, leading to their marriage when Dorabji was thirty-eight and Meherbai just eighteen. Together, Dorabji and Lady Meherbai shared a life dedicated to philanthropy and social reform.

Lady Meherbai Tata passed away on 18 June 1931 after a prolonged battle with leukaemia. Her death deeply affected Sir Dorabji Tata, who established the Meherbai Tata Memorial Trust in her memory to continue her legacy of supporting women's education and welfare. The trust focused on empowering women through various initiatives, such as scholarships for higher education and vocational training programs. Sir Dorabji passed away on 3 June 1932, nearly a year after Lady Meherbai breathed her last.

Ratanji Dadabhoy Tata, commonly known as R.D. Tata, was Jamsetji's first cousin. He was born in 1856 in Navsari, where he received his primary education before pursuing higher studies at Elphinstone College and later studying agricultural science in Madras (Chennai). After completing his education, he joined his father's company, Tata & Co., at a time when it was struggling to survive during an economic recession.

In 1883, R.D. took charge of the company and successfully navigated it through various hurdles. He was heavily involved in the establishment of Empress Mills in 1884 and later as a partner in Tata & Sons in 1887. Furthermore, he played a crucial role in the international expansion of the Tata business through the opening of branches in Shanghai, New York and Paris.

Following Jamsetji's death in 1907, R.D. Tata became a key partner in Tata & Sons and got involved in the iron and steel company, as well as the Indian Institute of Science. His leadership helped stabilize the company during World War I when the Tatas' business suffered monetary hardships. He was also actively involved in several welfare initiatives and served on the Imperial Legislative Council as an advocate for the iron and steel industry.

R.D. Tata received the Third Order of the Rising Sun from the Japanese emperor for enhancing trade relations between India

> The Indian Institute of Science (IISc), located in Bengaluru, is a leading institution for advanced education and research in science and engineering. Established on 27 May 1909, it was the brainchild of Jamsetji Nusserwanji Tata, who envisioned a world-class institute to promote scientific research in India. Inspired by a conversation with Swami Vivekananda, Jamsetji wanted to create an institution that would harbour innovation and contribute to the nation's development as a global leader in science and technology. To realize this vision, he collaborated with the Maharaja of Mysore, Krishnaraja Wodeyar IV, who generously donated 372 acres of land and provided financial support for the institute. Despite facing bureaucratic challenges, as well as his untimely death in 1904, Jamsetji's dream materialized with the support of the Mysore government and other stakeholders. IISc began with departments of general and applied chemistry, organic chemistry and electro-technology, welcoming its first batch of students in 1911. Over the years, it has grown into a leading research institution that continues to contribute to advancements in various fields, including engineering, biology and materials science.

and Japan. He passed away on 26 August 1926, leaving behind a legacy of industrial growth that would continue to be fostered by his successors.

Sir Ratan Tata, born on 20 January 1871, was the younger son of Jamsetji Tata and another significant member of the Tata family. He completed his education at St. Xavier's College in Bombay and married Navajbai Sett in 1892. After his father's death, Ratan began his career at a French insurance company associated with Tata & Sons and later managed various businesses within the family firm, including textiles and pearls. Although much of the responsibility for Tata & Sons fell on the shoulders of his elder brother, Dorabji, Ratan played a crucial role in land acquisitions in Mahim and Bandra.

A socially conscious individual, Sir Ratan was an ardent supporter of Mahatma Gandhi's efforts against British injustices in South Africa, and he contributed ₹1,25,000 to the cause. He also funded initiatives aimed at understanding and alleviating poverty, including a financial commitment to the University of London for research on social conditions. Furthermore, he facilitated the establishment of the Ratan Tata Department of Social Sciences at the London School of Economics. He was also an art enthusiast, known for his enviable collection of valuable artefacts procured during his travels, and his generosity was evident in his contributions to relief efforts during natural disasters and support for public institutions. Sir Ratan Tata passed away in September 1918 in England. His mausoleum is in Brookwood Cemetery, near that of his father, Jamsetji Tata.

Born in September 1877, **Navazbai Tata** was known for her philanthropy and leadership. She married Sir Ratan Tata in 1890, and the couple spent a part of their lives in London, where they gained respect among the British elite. An accomplished horse rider and polo player, Navajbai shared her husband's passion for fine art and contributed immensely to his collection. Widowed at the age of forty-one, Navajbai took on the responsibility of managing Sir Ratan's estate and was inducted as a director into the governing board of Tata Sons in

1918, becoming the first woman to hold such a position in the Tata Group. Her tenure lasted until her death in August 1965. Her philanthropy included several donations to the National Metallurgical Research Institute in Jamshedpur.

In 1928, she established the Ratan Tata Institute to provide training and employment opportunities to underprivileged women. As chairperson of the Sir Ratan Tata Trust, she invited S.J.I. Markham to assess and address the needs of the Parsi community through altruistic efforts. As she was childless, Navajbai adopted Naval Hormusji Tata, thereby ensuring the continuation of her husband's legacy, as well as the Tata family.

Naval Hormusji Tata, born on 30 August 1904 in Bombay, had humble origins, unlike his adoptive family. His birth family faced considerable hardships after the untimely death of his father, Hormusji Tata, a spinning master, when Naval was just four years old. Naval's widowed mother struggled to support her children through Zardozi work, leading to their eventual relocation to Surat. Due to the hardships the family faced, well-wishers arranged for Naval to stay at the J.N. Petit Parsi Orphanage, where he received his early education.

At the age of thirteen, Naval's life took a turn for the better when he was adopted by Lady Navajbai Tata. After studying economics and accountancy, he joined Tata Sons in 1930 as an assistant secretary. His career progressed rapidly – he became joint managing director of Tata Textiles in 1939 and later held various leadership roles across multiple sectors within the Tata Group.

Like other influential members of his family, Naval Tata was deeply involved in philanthropy, and also sports administration. He served as president of the Indian Cancer Society for nearly three decades and played a major role in promoting hockey in India as president of the Indian Hockey Federation. His commitment to labour relations was noteworthy; his advocacy for workers' rights was significant in the establishment of the National Institute of Labour Management.

Despite these achievements, Naval was known for his humility and kindness, as well as for engaging frequently with people from all walks of life. His dedication to social causes earned him the prestigious Padma Bhushan Award in 1969 for his contributions to industrial peace.

Naval's personal life included two marriages – first to Sooni Commissariat, with whom he had two sons – Ratan and Jimmy – and later to Simone Dunoyer, a Swiss national with whom he had another son, Noel. Following his divorce from Sooni in the 1940s, Lady Navajbai took over the responsibility of raising Ratan and Jimmy. Naval Hormusji Tata succumbed to cancer on 5 May 1989 in Bombay at the age of eighty-four.

Jehangir Ratanji Dadabhoy Tata, commonly known as J.R.D. Tata, was born on 29 July 1904 in Paris to Ratanji Dadabhoy Tata and Suzanne Brière. J.R.D. was a multifaceted individual who studied in several countries, including France and Japan, and he also briefly served in the French army. However, he returned to India in 1925 to join the family business, Tata & Sons, where he began his career as an assistant. By 1926, he was appointed as a director and ascended to the role of chairman in 1938 at just thirty-four years of age.

J.R.D. is celebrated as the father of civil aviation in India. He founded Tata Airlines in 1932, which later became Air India. He himself flew the airline's inaugural flight from Karachi to

Bombay in a De Havilland Puss Moth aircraft – a significant milestone in the history of Indian aviation. Under his leadership and till the time he retired in 1988, the Tata Group expanded dramatically from fourteen to ninety-five companies in various sectors such as steel, engineering and hospitality.

J.R.D. also established several institutions, such as the Tata Institute of Fundamental Research (along with Dr Homi Bhabha) and Tata Memorial Centre (then Tata Memorial Hospital). He founded the J.R.D. Tata Trust in 1944 to support sustainable social initiatives and facilitate family planning efforts. He received numerous accolades for his contributions, including the Bharat Ratna in 1992. He passed away on 29 November 1993 at the age of eighty-nine in Geneva, Switzerland, due to complications from a kidney infection.

Ratan Naval Tata: Formative Years and Education

Ratan Naval Tata was born on 28 December 1937 in Bombay to Naval Hormusji Tata and Sooni Tata, who came from a prominent Parsi Zoroastrian lineage. Although Ratan's early life was privileged, he also went through considerable upheaval due to his parents' divorce when he was just ten years old.

Following the separation of his parents, Ratan Tata and his younger brother, Jimmy, were raised by their paternal grandmother, Navazbai Tata, a formidable matriarch who instilled strong values and discipline in her grandchildren while providing a nurturing environment. Living in the opulent Tata Palace in Mumbai (then Bombay), Ratan's luxurious life was marred by the strict upbringing enforced by his grandmother. He once remarked, 'She was very indulgent, but also quite strict in terms of discipline.'

In addition to academic pursuits, Ratan was encouraged to learn the piano and play cricket, which became integral parts of his childhood. He recalled that their grandmother's protective nature limited their social interactions, and the brothers had a somewhat isolated upbringing: 'We were very protected and we didn't have many friends.'

School Years

Ratan Tata's early education began at the prestigious Campion School in Mumbai, where he faced the unique challenges of being a child from a highly affluent family. Although he excelled in academics, he encountered relentless bullying from peers, who envied his family's wealth. Reflecting on his school days and demonstrating a desire to fit in with his fellow students, Ratan noted, 'I remember that my grandmother used to have this huge antiquated Rolls-Royce... Both of us used to be so ashamed of that car that we used to walk back home.' He acknowledged the rigorous educational environment of the institution, stating, 'Most of us were forced to have tuitions... Life was quite a drudgery in those days.' Despite these challenges, he noted that certain experiences he perceived as burdensome later became his most cherished memories.

After completing his early education at Campion, Ratan Tata enrolled at the reputable Cathedral and John Connon School in Mumbai. This transition was significant for him, as Cathedral is famous for producing numerous notable alumni through its rigorous academic standards that prioritize holistic development.

At Cathedral, Ratan enjoyed friendships with students from diverse backgrounds – something that was lacking during his years at Campion. He later reflected on this experience, stating, 'None of us was flamboyant in those days, and it didn't matter whether you were rich or poor. There was a terrific amount of camaraderie.' Despite the school's demanding curriculum, Ratan found himself struggling with certain subjects. He once humorously recounted, 'I particularly remember a mathematics teacher who felt determined that I never complete school. He almost succeeded.' Regardless of his success in academics, Ratan struggled with shyness and a fear of public speaking. However, his experienced significant personal growth during his time at Cathedral, which ultimately prepared him for the future responsibilities he would undertake within the Tata Group.

Higher Education and Early Career

Ratan Tata enrolled in Cornell University in 1952, where he studied architecture and structural engineering, graduating in 1962. He described his time at Cornell as transformative, stating, 'The miles of tracing paper that all of us wasted on one concept after another taught us that we didn't stick with one thing. We tried and we tried, and we improved.' This approach to problem-solving became a hallmark of his later business strategies.

During his time at Cornell, he not only honed his academic skills but also developed a passion for design and innovation. His architectural training helped him develop a creative mindset that he credited for some of his future successes in business. In a documentary produced for his fiftieth reunion, he reflected on how the principles learned during these years helped him approach challenges: 'It's no different in business.'

Beyond academics, Ratan Tata devoted himself to the rich

campus life at Cornell and joined the Alpha Sigma Phi fraternity, which provided him with a sense of community in a foreign land. His love for flying also flourished during this period, and he is known to have once executed an emergency landing of a four-seater aircraft that suffered engine failure with classmates onboard.

Ratan Tata's connection to Cornell extended well beyond his student years. As a former trustee and the university's largest international donor, he made several financial contributions that have had lasting impacts on education and research at the university. In 2008, he helped to establish the Tata-Cornell Institute for Agriculture and Nutrition with a $25 million endowment. Likewise, in 2017, he funded the Tata Innovation Center on Cornell Tech's Roosevelt Island campus with a $50 million investment to encourage collaboration between academia and industry.

Ratan Tata's legacy at Cornell is further exhibited in the values he championed – creativity, problem-solving and social responsibility. As noted by Michael I. Kotlikoff, interim president of Cornell University, 'Ratan's quiet demeanor and humility belied his international profile. His generosity and concern for others enabled research and scholarship that improved the education and health of millions.'

When he returned to India in late 1962, Ratan Tata joined the Tata Group, thus beginning his career as an assistant working on the shop floor of Tata Industries in Jamshedpur. Under the mentorship of J.R.D. Tata, who was chairman of the Tata Group at the time, Ratan immersed himself in various aspects of steel production, engaging in hands-on work alongside other employees. This foundational period was important as it provided him with insights into the Tata Group's operational intricacies.

In 1963, Ratan Tata joined the Tata Iron and Steel Company (TISCO), now known as Tata Steel, at its Jamshedpur facility. His dedication and aptitude quickly caught the attention of senior management, leading to his appointment as a technical officer in Tata Steel's engineering division in 1965. This role allowed Tata to gain hands-on experience in the steel industry.

Seeking to gain international exposure, Tata took on the role of the Tata Group's resident representative in Australia in 1969. This position provided him with valuable insights into global business practices and helped him develop a more comprehensive perspective on the Tata Group's potential for international expansion. After his stint in Australia, he returned to India in 1970, briefly joining Tata Consultancy Services (TCS), which was then a fledgling software company. His time at TCS, though short, exposed him to the emerging field of information technology, which would later play a crucial role in the Tata Group's diversification.

In 1971, Ratan Tata faced the first of his major work-related challenges when he was appointed director-in-charge of the National Radio and Electronics Company (NELCO). At that time, NELCO was struggling financially, with many stakeholders doubting its potential for recovery. Despite the scepticism surrounding the company's survival, Ratan demonstrated remarkable foresight and successfully convinced J.R.D. Tata to invest further in NELCO despite the latter's reluctance. Ratan's leadership during this tumultuous period laid the groundwork for his future management style. He famously recalled, 'Those 8 or 10 years in NELCO were what I drew upon in later years.' His commitment to understanding the intricacies of labour relations was made evident by his frequent interactions with workers' unions to address their concerns. Under his guidance, NELCO began to recover against all odds, with its market share increasing from 2 per cent to 20 per cent between 1972 and 1975.

However, some challenges persisted. The declaration of a national emergency in 1975 led to a recession and subsequent strikes, which severely impacted NELCO's financial performance. Ratan's experiences at NELCO taught him critical lessons about managing crises and granted him extensive knowledge of market dynamics. While many perceived NELCO's struggles as failures, Ratan recognized them as opportunities for his growth and learning, remarking years later that the challenges during this period shaped his personal approach to leadership.

His commitment to self-improvement led him back to academia; his educational journey continued at Harvard Business School (HBS) in 1975, where he enrolled in the Advanced Management Program. Upon his arrival, Ratan was overwhelmed by the impressive accomplishments of his classmates, which led to feelings of confusion and humiliation. He candidly shared, 'It was the only time in my life where I sat and crossed out day-by-day how many days were left before I could return to the normal world.' Nevertheless, he recognized the profound impact of his time at Harvard, later reflecting, 'As I look back, those 13 weeks were probably the most important 13 weeks of my life. They transformed me and my perspective.' At HBS, he learned to appreciate the abundance of knowledge available at the prestigious institution, stating, 'The confusion sort of disappeared, and you understood the magnitude of what you had learned in a manner that I believe is not possible to do in places other than at this business school.'

Harvard Business School building in Cambridge, Massachusetts, USA

Ratan Tata's time at Harvard not only equipped him with essential management skills but also reinforced his belief in continuous learning and adaptability – qualities that would become definitive traits of his leadership style.

In the early 1950s, amidst concerns about foreign exchange outflow due to imported cosmetics, Prime Minister Jawaharlal Nehru encouraged J.R.D. Tata to establish an indigenous Indian cosmetics brand. This led to the creation of Lakmé, named after the French opera 'Lakmé' and inspired by Lakshmi, the Hindu goddess of beauty and wealth. Lakmé, launched with the tagline 'If colour be to beauty what music is to mood, play on', began as a 100% subsidiary of Tata Oil Mills Company (TOMCO) and initially operated from a small rented space in Bombay. Simone Tata, wife of Naval Tata and Ratan Tata's stepmother, joined the brand as director in 1961 and came to play a pivotal role in Lakmé's growth, ultimately becoming chairperson in 1982. Under her leadership, Lakmé expanded its product range, opened its first branded beauty salon in 1980, and became synonymous with Indian beauty. Recognizing the need for cosmetics tailored to Indian skin tones and climate, she spearheaded the introduction of the popular 'Enrich Lipsticks', which came in an array of shades, alongside a wide spectrum of nail polish colours. The brand later also ventured into skincare, introducing moisturisers designed for Indian weather conditions and sun protection products. Simone Tata also oversaw the establishment of a robust product development process involving rigorous testing and research to ensure products met safety and quality standards. Lakmé's innovative marketing strategies were highly successful, including the iconic 'Lakmé girl' campaigns featuring Shyamoli Verma, who went on to become India's first supermodel. Over the years, several prominent Bollywood actresses like Rekha, Aishwarya Rai Bachchan and Kareena Kapoor Khan have also featured in Lakmé ad campaigns. This combination of targeted product development, quality assurance and culturally relevant marketing helped the brand penetrate and thrive in the Indian market. In 1996, it entered a 50:50 joint venture with Hindustan Unilever (HUL); and by 1998, the Tatas sold their stake for ₹200 crore. Today, Lakmé remains one of the market leaders in India's cosmetics industry.

Lakme cosmetics display for sale in Kuala Lumpur, Malaysia

Nusserwanji Tata (3 March 1839– 19 May 1904)

Dorabji Tata (27 August 1859– 3 June 1932)

Naval Hormusji Tata (30 August 1904– 5 May 1989)

Tatanagar Station, Jharkhand, India

CHAPTER 2

ENTRY INTO THE TATA GROUP

- Joining the Family Business
- Evolution of Leadership Skills

Joining the Family Business

In chapter 1, we have already had glimpses of Ratan Tata's formative years and how and when he was introduced to his family business. Here we will start from his National Radio and Electronics Company (NELCO) days.

Years at NELCO

In 1974, Ratan Tata joined the board of Tata Sons as a director, which further solidified his influence within the group. His focus on fostering new technologies and streamlining operations was crucial as efforts to liberalize the Indian economy began in the late 1980s. Ratan's leadership style emphasized collaboration and inclusivity, allowing him to build strong relationships with key stakeholders. However, the following year was a turbulent one for him, a year marred by the significant challenges he faced as director-in-charge at NELCO. Ratan had initially been successful in turning the struggling company around by helping its market share increase considerably. However, the declaration of a national emergency in India under the Indira Gandhi-led Congress government that year led to a severe economic downturn that adversely impacted NELCO's financial performance. The consequent recession resulted in labour strikes and operational disruptions that threatened the stability he had worked hard to achieve.

During this period, Ratan Tata attempted to shift NELCO's focus towards industrial electronics primarily due to a lack of capital and limited support from Tata Power, which owned NELCO. Although Ratan Tata remained committed to NELCO's potential, the company struggled to secure adequate capital for expansion, largely because Tata Power showed little interest in consumer electronics.

Recalling the difficulties of this period, Ratan noted a time when NELCO had been yet again on the brink of collapse. He was facing cash flow issues during this period and was often unsure if he would be able to meet payroll requirements. This situation forced him to borrow money from banks to keep the company afloat. Despite these setbacks, Ratan believed this experience to have been a crucial learning opportunity. Years later, he stated that it taught him valuable lessons about handling labour relations and crisis management.

Chairmanship of Tata Industries and the Tata Strategic Plan

In 1974, Ratan also joined the board of Tata Sons as a director, and his involvement in various company initiatives allowed him to gain insights into the broader operations of the conglomerate. In 1977, Ratan Tata was given the responsibility of reviving Empress Mills. This Tata Group entity was facing severe financial difficulties and operational inefficiencies. He encountered substantial resistance from senior management regarding his proposed revitalization plan, which included a crucial investment of ₹50 lakh for modernizing the facility's infrastructure. Unfortunately, the management's refusal to approve this investment led to the mill's 1986 takeover by the Maharashtra State Textile Corporation, which ultimately closed the mill in 2002. This experience deepened Ratan Tata's understanding of corporate restructuring and the importance of securing buy-in from stakeholders. While the failure of Empress Mills was disheartening for Tata, it also instilled in him a resilience that lasted his entire life.

In 1981, Ratan was appointed chairman of Tata Industries. As chairman, Ratan Tata immediately began the process of transforming Tata Industries into a promoter of high-technology businesses. Ratan recognized that Tata Group's future depended on adapting to market dynamics, and in 1983, he drafted the Tata Strategic Plan – a comprehensive plan for the company, outlining his vision for diversifying and expanding the business into emerging sectors. While some within the organization expressed uncertainty about venturing into high-tech industries, Ratan Tata remained resolute. He argued that large groups like Tata had the capacity to take calculated risks in pursuing new business avenues.

Ratan Tata's detailed roadmap resulted in the conglomerate moving away from its traditional reliance on legacy businesses and entering emerging sectors like telecommunications, biotechnology and advanced materials. At a time when India was still largely under the constraints of the Licence Raj, Ratan foresaw a shift towards a more liberalized economy and had conviction in the advantages of leveraging the group's size and diversity to harbour collaboration among its various companies. The plan proposed increasing ownership stakes in group companies to foster a more unified corporate identity that would enable Tata to operate as a cohesive entity rather than a loose conglomeration of independent firms. Consequently, his plan culminated in the systemic promotion of seven key ventures – Tata Telecom, Tata Finance, Tata Keltron, Hitech Drilling Services, Tata Honeywell, Tata Elxsi and Plantek.

In 1989, a massive labour dispute occurred at TELCO. The conflict was led by trade unionist Rajan Nair, who was the working president of the Telco Kamgar Sanghatna union. The dispute culminated in a hunger strike at Shaniwarwada in 1989. For three days, the entire industrial belt of Pune joined the strike in support, marking an important moment in trade union history. The dispute originated from disagreements over wage revisions, with Nair having been suspended in 1983 after a previous dispute on the same issue. To address the crisis, the then chief minister Sharad Pawar arranged a meeting between Nair and Ratan Tata. Despite being new to his role, Ratan Tata demonstrated an understanding of the issues at hand, listening to the concerns and treating Nair as an equal, as reported by Nair in later years. Ratan maintained his position throughout the dispute, and ultimately, the resolution favoured the company. Reflecting on this experience in a later interview, Tata expressed his appreciation for his role at TELCO, referring to it as 'the first company in which I could actually do something. In other companies, I was always put in a fire-fighting situation'.

Implementing these ambitious initiatives was not an easy task.

Ratan's vision for modernization often clashed with the strong personalities of various CEOs, who often operated autonomously while leading these companies. Some of these CEOs reportedly ignored Tata's plans frequently. Most notably, Russi Mody, who was the chairman of Tata Steel at the time. Mody's independent management style and resistance to Ratan's strategic direction created friction.

The relationship between Ratan Tata and Russi Mody became even more strained in early 1992 when Ratan revived an existing policy that mandated a retirement age of sixty-five years for executive directors, including managing directors and executive chairmen, whereas non-executive directors were required to retire at seventy-five years. This policy was part of Ratan's broader strategy to consolidate power and modernize the group. At the time, Mody was seventy-four and complied with the policy by stepping down from his executive role and transitioning to the position of non-executive chairman of Tata Steel. However, as his retirement approached, tensions with the Tata Steel board and Ratan Tata escalated to the point that they often spilled into the public domain.

Mody openly criticized Ratan's leadership style and questioned the motives behind the retirement policy. He famously likened Ratan to a circus performer, predicting dire consequences for the group if such changes were implemented. Despite this resistance, Ratan remained steadfast. Their conflict reached a critical juncture when Mody appointed his adopted son, Aditya Kashyap, as deputy managing director without securing board approval, a decision that greatly irked Ratan. When Mody sought intervention from political figures, including Prime Minister P.V. Narasimha Rao and Finance Minister Manmohan Singh, he was met with refusal. To resolve this conflict, J.R.D. Tata intervened, as he had been a mentor to both men. He reminded Mody of the need for collective decision-making and respect for the board's authority. Ultimately, under pressure from Ratan and J.R.D., Mody was compelled to withdraw Kashyap's promotion, with both Mody and Kashyap exiting the company.

Several years later, Ratan expressed his frustration, stating, 'I don't understand why Russi behaved the way he did. He was my friend. He was Jeh's (J.R.D.'s) favourite. But he just became totally unreasonable.' This conflict is an example of the broader struggle Ratan faced in initially asserting his leadership.

Another significant feud occurred with Darbari Seth, chairman of Tata Chemicals and Tata Tea. Seth publicly stated that 'the Tata Group is a commonwealth of enterprises, not an empire', reflecting the sentiment of many CEOs who were protective of their independence. This sentiment often meant that Ratan's novel ideas were sidelined or blatantly ignored, creating friction between him and the established leadership. This lack of alignment with Ratan's goals hindered the group's ability to adapt to changing market conditions and embrace new opportunities.

The discord reached a critical point with Ratan Tata's 1992 retirement policy. As a result, Seth was compelled to step down from his position in 1994; however, before his departure, he appointed his son, Manu Seth, as managing director, although Manu would resign in 2000 due to 'differences in professional perception'.

Tata's modernization strategy proved to be fruitful as India began to liberalize its economy in the early 1990s to counter a severe economic crisis in the nation. A key feature of these

Tata Chemicals Winnington Plant, Chesire, England

reforms was the removal of restrictive licencing and regulations that had previously hampered business expansion, which allowed Tata companies to operate with greater autonomy. Moreover, the liberalization policies enabled foreign direct investment, which opened avenues for strategic partnerships and collaborations. Ratan Tata was quick to recognize the potential benefits of this new economic landscape, stating, 'We were too conservative about liberalization before 1991... but we tried to change when the market opened.'

> **RATAN IS OFTEN BOTH PRAISED AND CRITICIZED FOR SAYING 'I DON'T BELIEVE IN TAKING RIGHT DECISIONS, I TAKE DECISIONS AND MAKE THEM RIGHT.' HOWEVER, WHEN HE WAS ASKED TO SHED LIGHT ON THE STATEMENT AT AN EVENT, TATA SAID, 'I AM SORRY TO UPSET YOU, BUT IT'S A STATEMENT MADE BY FACEBOOK OR TWITTER.'**

Later, in 1991, when Ratan assumed the chairmanship of the Tata Group following J.R.D. Tata's long tenure, he dusted off the 1983 strategic plan he had helped draft and adapted it for the even more liberalized economy of the time.

Leadership of Air India and Tata Steel

In September 1986, Ratan Tata's career hit another milestone when he was appointed the chairman of Air India. This role came at a critical time for the airline as it was grappling with operational and financial inefficiencies. It was during this time that his leadership style finally began to gain recognition and respect within the industry. Nonetheless, the challenges that Air India had been facing did not have easy fixes. The airline faced intense competition from private carriers that were entering the market, which put additional pressure on its operations. Despite these obstacles, Ratan advocated for internal reforms for the airline's success.

During Ratan's tenure at Air India, which lasted until 1989, he implemented several key reforms aimed at revitalizing the airline and restoring its reputation. One of the first initiatives he undertook was enhancing the quality of service. He believed in the importance of customer experience, stating, 'We must treat our passengers as guests, not just customers.' This philosophy led to improvements in cabin crew training and grooming standards.

Additionally, Ratan Tata focused on upgrading the fleet. He recognized that outdated aircraft posed a significant drawback to the airline's competitiveness. Under his leadership, Air India began acquiring new aircraft, which not only improved operational efficiency but also enhanced passenger comfort, thereby positioning Air India as a viable competitor in both domestic and international markets. Tata's plan also included prioritizing operational efficiency by implementing better scheduling practices and improving on-time performance. He understood that reliability was essential for regaining customer trust and loyalty in the airline and worked on strengthening its financial position by revising the existing cost structures.

In 1985, Ratan Tata took on a new leadership role as deputy chairman of Tata Steel. This transition was not without its difficulties due to Tata's conflict-riddled relationship with Mody, a formidable figure within the company. However, by 1988, Ratan had firmly established himself as a key figure within the conglomerate and earned immense respect for his forward-thinking approach.

Ratan Tata took on the leadership at Tata Steel with intense conviction and foresight and initiated several rounds of painful restructuring to align the company with modern standards. After assuming the chairmanship, one of his primary focuses was on streamlining the production processes. He believed that adopting new technologies was essential for enhancing production capabilities and improving efficiency. This vision led to substantial investments in advanced manufacturing technologies, which included upgrading existing facilities and introducing state-of-the-art equipment. As Ratan Tata himself stated, 'We must not only be competitive but also be leaders in technology.' He also understood the necessity of operational efficiency and implemented rigorous performance metrics and accountability measures to streamline the company's operations.

One of the measures undertaken under Tata's restructuring drive was workforce reduction, which was contentious yet necessary. The steel industry was facing overcapacity issues, and Tata Steel had to adapt to remain viable. By 1991, the company workforce had reduced significantly from over 100,000 employees to less than half that number. This decision was not made lightly, and Ratan demonstrated empathy for his employees during this process, stating, 'We must handle change with care and compassion.' The restructuring efforts involved adopting humane practices, ensuring that employees who were let go received adequate support and re-training opportunities.

Ratan Tata also prioritized improving corporate governance within Tata Steel. He established clearer lines of accountability and encouraged transparency in decision-making processes – a shift that he believed was essential for promoting trust among employees and stakeholders. By requiring subsidiaries to report directly to the group office, Ratan wanted to create a more cohesive organizational structure. Under his leadership, Tata Steel began exploring international markets and forming strategic alliances.

The reforms implemented by Ratan Tata had a profound impact

on Tata Steel's financial performance. By focusing on operational efficiency and modernization, the company improved its profitability and competitiveness. Analysts noted that these changes positioned Tata Steel favourably against its peers in the industry. Ratan's novel approach earned him immense respect within the organization and got him the reputation of a leader who could navigate challenges without compromising on excellence. Under his guidance, Tata Steel began to emerge as a more agile and competitive player in the steel industry. Throughout this period, Ratan Tata demonstrated resilience and strategic foresight with a commendable ability to navigate complex corporate dynamics.

Philanthropic Initiatives through the Sir Ratan Tata Trust

After demonstrating his enviable business acumen that enabled him to successfully steer the company through several challenges, in 1989, Ratan Tata also took charge of the Sir Ratan Tata Trust. This philanthropic organization was established in 1919 with a focus on social welfare and community development. Under Ratan's leadership, the trust intensified its efforts to address several pressing social issues across India.

Ratan Tata at Maharaja Lakshman Sen Memorial College, Sundernagar, Himachal Pradesh

The most important charitable initiative he undertook during this period was utilizing the trust's resources to enhance the livelihoods of and impart education to people residing in rural areas, as well as those from marginalized communities. The Sir Ratan Tata Trust provided grants to various organizations engaged in groundbreaking projects aimed at improving the quality of life for vulnerable individuals. This included support for educational institutions, healthcare programmes and initiatives focused on women's empowerment. Ratan believed that education and skill development were crucial for long-term societal progress. Additionally, the trust expanded its focus on health-related initiatives, funding programmes that improved access to medical care and promoted public health awareness. This included partnerships with organizations that addressed critical health issues like maternal and child health, nutrition and disease prevention.

In 1998, Ratan Tata launched the Sir Ratan Tata Small Grants Programme (SGP), designed to support small, welfare-oriented organizations in India. It would provide financial assistance to grassroots entities and community-based projects tackling social issues that had previously lacked access to larger funds and resources. To qualify for a grant under the SGP, organizations needed to have been operational for at least one financial year with an annual expenditure not exceeding ₹2 million and a workforce of no more than twenty employees. This structure ensured that the programme catered specifically to smaller organizations, thereby empowering them to implement impactful projects without the burden of extensive bureaucratic requirements.

Since its inception, the SGP continues to support countless establishments across various thematic areas, including education, health, rural livelihoods and civil society. It has played a crucial role in field-testing new ideas and pilot projects that could later be scaled or integrated into larger initiatives. By focusing on sustainable development and social responsibility, Ratan Tata positioned the Sir Ratan Tata Trust as a significant player in India's corporate philanthropic scene.

Ratan was known for his visionary thinking, which he employed to steer the Tata Group through periods of considerable turmoil. Another major aspect of how he led his businesses was his deep sense of empathy and a people-centric approach to problem-solving. From early on in his career, he focused on building strong relationships with employees at all levels, making individuals working with him feel valued and empowered. As an advocate for innovation and creativity, Ratan was known for encouraging a work culture in which employees felt motivated to think outside the box and pursue groundbreaking ideas. This was evident in projects like the Tata Nano, which aimed to provide affordable transportation solutions for millions in India. Furthermore, Ratan valued diverse perspectives, encouraging collaboration, open dialogue and shared ownership of outcomes.

Throughout his illustrious career, Ratan faced numerous challenges such as economic downturns and intense competition. His ability to remain stable during tough times has been a hallmark of his leadership style. Coming from a family of compassionate philanthropists, Ratan Tata firmly believed that businesses have a responsibility to contribute positively to society. His commitment to corporate social responsibility (CSR) was reflected in the community development and environmental sustainability projects that started under his leadership, with the Tata Group quickly establishing itself as one of the leaders in ethical business practices.

Evolution of
Leadership Skills

1975–1992

Ratan Tata's leadership skills evolved significantly during this period. It was personally transformative for him as he navigated various challenges and opportunities. His early appointment as the director-in-charge of NELCO in 1971 greatly shaped his resilience and strategic thinking as he learned to manage crises and adapt to changing market conditions.

1975

Ratan's completion of the advanced management programme at Harvard Business School helped refine his management acumen and exposed him to new business concepts and leadership strategies that reportedly influenced his business decision-making style.

1981

Ratan Tata was appointed chairman of Tata Industries, where the strategic plan for the company that he drafted and implemented in 1983 exemplified his ability to think critically outside the traditional business norms prevalent in India at the time.

1986–1989

His time as chairman of Air India further sharpened his skills in managing large companies. Later, after his appointment as chairman of Tata Steel in 1987, he faced the challenge of revitalizing one of India's oldest industrial enterprises. Ratan Tata's leadership during this period was characterized by a commitment to restructuring operations and investing in new technologies.

Throughout this early period in his career, Ratan Tata's leadership style matured into one personified by collaboration, inclusivity and long-term vision. He cultivated relationships with key stakeholders across the Tata Group, creating an environment in which innovation could thrive. As he prepared to succeed J.R.D. Tata, Ratan realized that India was on the cusp of economic liberalization and began discussions about diversifying the Tata Group's portfolio into new sectors and markets.

1992 Shortly after assuming leadership of the Tata Group, Ratan began several initiatives to enhance brand value and corporate identity on a global scale. He oversaw the launch of new products under various Tata brands while also establishing partnerships with international firms to foster innovation and technology transfer. His commitment to sustainable business practices became evident as he advocated for corporate social responsibility initiatives aligned with Tata's philanthropic legacy.

Ratan Tata at the AeroIndia Airshow in Bengaluru , Karnataka, India

Tribal artists performing at Samvaad *2016 – a tribal conclave organised by Tata Steel , Jamshedpur, Jharkhand. The annual event started on 15 November 2014 to commemorate the birth anniversary of the tribal leader Birsa Munda. It was the first tribal conclave by an Indian corporate house.*

Ratan Tata Quotes

As days go by, I will begin to focus my attention on specific areas where value can be added to enhance the quality of life of the rural citizens.

CHAPTER 3

RISE TO CHAIRMANSHIP

- Becoming the Chairman
- Strategic Leadership and Expansion
- Investment in Research and Development Across Industries

Becoming Chairman

Jehangir Ratanji Dadabhoy Tata (29 July 1904–29 November 1993)

In March 1991, a significant leadership transition occurred within the Tata Group as the legendary chairman J.R.D. Tata stepped down after a celebrated tenure spanning over five decades. In a historic decision, he named Ratan Tata as his successor, thus heralding a new era for the conglomerate in which it flourished vastly more than it had previously.

J.R.D. had been a guiding force in shaping the Tata Group into one of

India's most respected business houses, and his endorsement of Ratan was a testament to the latter's readiness to take on this enormous responsibility. J.R.D.'s decision to name Ratan Tata as his successor was influenced by a combination of personal circumstances and the evolving needs of the group. In the late 1980s, J.R.D. Tata faced several health challenges, including heart disease, which prompted him to prepare for retirement and assign a successor. During this period, Ratan Tata began developing a closer relationship with J.R.D., particularly in the last six years of his life. This connection was pivotal in J.R.D.'s decision regarding the succession.

Initially, Ratan was not seen as a frontrunner for leadership, and other executives like Russi Mody and Darbari Seth were considered more likely candidates. However, J.R.D. believed that the Tata Group needed someone from within the family to maintain its legacy and cohesion during a time of change. Ultimately, J.R.D. recognized Ratan's potential and commitment to the group, leading him to officially name Ratan as his heir during a poignant moment after being admitted to the Breach Candy Hospital in 1991. More than two years later, on 29 November 1993, J.R.D. succumbed to his health issues, particularly a severe kidney infection, and passed away in Geneva at the age of 89.

This transition was not merely a change of leadership within the group, it represented a generational shift within the Tata family, as well as in the broader corporate landscape. Ratan was aware of the weight of expectations placed upon him as the chairman, and he was knowingly stepping into shoes that had long been associated with visionary leadership and innovation, which has been studied in business schools. He later stated, 'I followed someone who had very large shoes. He left me a great legacy, and I tried to follow that legacy.' The timing of the changing leadership also happened to coincide with the peak of India's economic liberalization, which presented both challenges and opportunities for Ratan as he prepared to steer the conglomerate.

Following J.R.D. Tata's retirement in 1991, Ratan Tata officially assumed the role of chairman of Tata Sons and the Tata Trusts. Ratan knew that the values instilled by his predecessors were vital to maintaining the integrity and reputation of the Tata brand as it evolved. Thus, his leadership began with a continued focus on restructuring and modernizing the group to adapt to the rapidly changing economic scene in India. Ratan's approach encompassed expanding the group's global footprint while adhering to its foundational principles of ethical business practices and social responsibility. Under his stewardship, the Tata Trusts also continued their commitment to philanthropy with an emphasis on education, healthcare and rural development.

In 1991, Ratan Tata initiated a comprehensive restructuring of the Tata Group. With the knowledge that the traditional business models that had been prominent in India were becoming obsolete in a globally competitive environment, he sought to upgrade operations across various subsidiaries. This restructuring involved streamlining processes, measures to enhance overall productivity and fostering innovation within each company. He understood that adapting to global market dynamics required a major cultural shift within the organization, and therefore he encouraged collaboration among different business units under Tata, as well as cross-functional teams. Furthermore, his approach included investing in research and development and encouraging employees to adopt a culture of continuous improvement.

However, despite his extensive experience within the Tata

Group, Ratan Tata faced the intense scepticism of industry peers regarding his leadership capabilities. Many questioned whether he could uphold the legacy established by J.R.D. and effectively lead a conglomerate that had grown to vast proportions since its inception. Several critics pointed out his limited experience in certain sectors compared to seasoned executives who had been entrenched in the industries for decades. Nonetheless, Ratan remained undeterred by those doubts. He went on to have an eminent career that gained him worldwide reverence and proved his detractors wrong.

Under his guidance, various subsidiaries began investing in research and development and forming partnerships with technology firms, as well as academic institutions, to facilitate education. Under Ratan Tata's leadership, in 1991, the Tata Group began significantly expanding its international presence as part of its strategic vision for growth. Recognizing that globalization offered immense opportunities for Indian businesses, he initiated efforts to enter new markets beyond India's borders. This expansion included exploring acquisitions and partnerships with foreign companies that could enhance Tata's capabilities and product offerings. Ratan's approach was characterized by careful market analysis and strategic investments aimed at establishing a foothold in key regions around the world.

In chapter 2 we have already discussed Ratan Tata's implementation of a retirement policy for senior executives in 1991, which was aimed at bringing fresh talent into key positions across various subsidiaries. Understanding that innovation often requires new perspectives, he believed that introducing younger leaders could invigorate organizational culture and drive change more effectively. The introduction of this policy was perceived as a radical shift from traditional practices, wherein long-serving executives held onto their positions for as long as possible. By encouraging retirement among senior leaders who had served for decades, Ratan aimed to create space for new ideas and approaches from younger leaders that would align with his drive for transformation.

In the same year, as part of his commitment to enhancing corporate governance within the Tata Group, Ratan Tata instituted several other reforms, one of which required subsidiaries to report directly to Tata Sons rather than through intermediary layers of management. This move was made to increase accountability among subsidiary leaders and promote additional transparency throughout the organization. By streamlining the reporting structures, he wanted to ensure that strategic decisions were made in alignment with overall group objectives while enabling quicker responses to the ever-changing market trends. This emphasis on corporate governance demonstrated his understanding that strong oversight was crucial for maintaining integrity within the diversified conglomerate that Tata Sons had become while reinforcing stakeholder confidence in its operations.

Under Ratan Tata's leadership, in 1991–92, the Tata Group launched several new products and services across various subsidiary companies. This period also saw the introduction of groundbreaking offerings to cater to evolving consumer needs. Most notably, Tata Motors entered the passenger vehicle market with models like the Tata Sierra and Tata Estate in a significant milestone for the company. Additionally, Tata Tea expanded its product line by introducing new blends that appealed to a broader audience. These launches firmly placed Tata brands as household names in India. Ratan's focus on

A 2020 Tata Sierra model

product development underscored his belief in continuous improvement and customer satisfaction, which became central tenets of the Tata Group's ethos. Therefore, knowing that cultivating a strong brand identity was essential, he began unifying the diverse portfolio of companies under a cohesive identity. This involved implementing standardized branding strategies and promoting a consistent image across all Tata entities. His initiatives included the creation of a single logo for all Tata companies, as well as stringent brand management practices. By fostering a strong corporate identity, Ratan aimed to elevate the Tata brand on the global stage.

Ratan also launched partnerships with international firms to foster state-of-the-art technology transfer to the Tata Group. For example, Tata Motors engaged in joint ventures with international automotive manufacturers to leverage their expertise in vehicle design and production.

As part of its strategy for global expansion, Ratan Tata also began to explore established businesses suitable for acquisition. He knew that strategic acquisitions would provide immediate access to new technologies, markets and expertise while strengthening the group's competitive edge. This approach was particularly important as India opened up to foreign investment and competition following its economic reforms of 1991. Ratan's strategy involved identifying underperforming companies with strong potential for turnaround or those that complemented existing Tata businesses. His proactive stance on acquisitions laid the groundwork for significant growth in subsequent years, which further diversified the group's portfolio.

Alongside the expansion drive, Ratan Tata also became an advocate for sustainable business practices within the group's operations through prioritization of environmental stewardship and social responsibility across all business units. Under his leadership, multiple initiatives were launched for reducing waste, conserving resources and promoting sustainable development within communities impacted by Tata operations. Ratan believed that integrating sustainability into business strategies would enhance consumer trust in the company's undertakings. His commitment to sustainability was novel for its time and set a precedent within the Indian industrial landscape, ultimately resulting in the Tata Group becoming a leader in corporate social responsibility (CSR). Tata formalized a framework for CSR that aligned with the conglomerate's legacy of philanthropic initiatives. This framework centred around community engagement, education, healthcare, ethical business practices and environmental sustainability as its core pillars.

Strategic Leadership and Expansion

Ratan Tata's strategic leadership and ability to turn a difficult situation into his favour gave him a legendary status in Indian industry.

Entry into the passenger vehicle market

Under Ratan's leadership, Tata Motors made a significant leap into the passenger vehicle market with the 1991 launch of Tata Sierra – India's first off-road SUV – in a bold move that diversified the company's portfolio. Steered by Ratan, this venture aimed to redefine the automotive landscape in India. The Sierra's entry into the Indian automobile market was followed by that of the iconic Tata Indica in 1998. Though the initial

> At the launch of Tata Indica, Ratan Tata announced, 'This is the first passenger car designed and developed entirely in India. We have developed a car that is truly Indian in its conception.'

Tata Indica, India's first passenger car designed and manufactured entirely in India

response was inspiring, very soon it met with sharp criticism from the users – to the extent of customers turning violent at certain locations. In 2000–01, sales dropped at an alarming rate, causing Tata Motors to register a loss of ₹500 crore that year.

After the debacle, Tata Motors, under the leadership of Ratan Tata, repaired over forty-five thousand cars in various retro camps, changing at least forty-two parts in each at the company's cost. This was the time when they also came back with an all-new Indica V2, in 2001. The turnaround had only begun. The next eighteen months saw a staggering sale of 1,00,00 Indica cars and Tata Motors posting a growth of 46 per cent that year.

The success of Indica compelled competitors like Maruti Suzuki to adjust their pricing strategies. The Indica's unique value proposition of offering Ambassador-like spaciousness at a Maruti 800-like price forced Tata's rivals to reassess their product positioning and pricing structures. Maruti Suzuki responded by reducing the price of its M800 model and accelerating the development of new offerings, including diesel variants, to compete with the Indica's pioneering small diesel engine. The Indica's success, underpinned by its 'More car per car' and Indica V2's 'Even more car per car' marketing campaigns and high level of indigenous components, prompted other automobile companies to innovate in their marketing approaches, reconsider their supply chains and invest more heavily in local research and development.

THIS STORY OF RATAN TATA'S ABILITY TO TURN INITIAL FAILURE INTO RESOUNDING SUCCESS, WITHOUT BEING BOGGED DOWN EITHER BY FINANCIAL LOSSES OR BY OVERWHELMINGLY ACRIMONIOUS PUBLIC REACTION, WILL CONTINUE TO INSPIRE BUSINESSES FOR AGES.

International partnerships

The liberalization policies introduced in 1991 opened several avenues for Tata to make foreign investments and compete in an international market. To finance these ambitious ventures, Ratan Tata embarked on significant financial manoeuvres. Notably, he sold a 20 per cent stake in Tata Industries Ltd. to Hong Kong-based Jardine Matheson Group for approximately $35 million. He remarked years later, in 2013, 'We were too conservative about the liberalization but tried to adapt when market was opened in 1991. [...] We, however, did better compared to other companies in the open market.'

Some of the key partnerships established by the Tata Group during Ratan Tata's tenure as chairman are listed below.

1. Singapore Airlines

Ratan Tata began conducting exploratory discussions with Singapore Airlines (SIA), a renowned carrier that had earned worldwide success, to establish airline services in India, a move that he hoped would successfully combine Tata's deep understanding of the Indian market with SIA's world-class aviation expertise. However, the collaboration between Tata and SIA was not without its initial challenges. When they first attempted to launch a joint venture airline in India in 1994, their effort was met with significant opposition from various quarters, including politicians, bureaucrats and competing airlines. The proposal had initially suggested SIA holding a 60 per cent stake and Tata taking the remaining 40 per cent. However, many politicians and bureaucrats were concerned about a foreign entity holding a majority stake in an Indian carrier and were hesitant to approve such a significant foreign investment in the sensitive aviation sector. Furthermore, existing private carriers, particularly Jet Airways, lobbied against the proposal due to fears of tough competition from a well-funded world-class airline. Ratan Tata made renewed attempts in 1996 to secure the partnership, even offering to switch the proposed shareholding stakes to address concerns about foreign control. Nonetheless, the deal failed to materialize, largely due to opposition from the then civil aviation minister and other political figures. The partnership faced another hurdle in 2001 when the government decided against state participation in civil aviation. Tata and SIA emerged as the sole bidders for a 40 per cent stake in Air India. However, this attempt, too, was thwarted by strong opposition from labour unions and rival airlines.

Vistara

Despite these setbacks, Ratan Tata's vision for a world-class Indian airline remained unwavering. The persistent efforts of Tata and SIA finally bore fruit in 2013 when they received regulatory approval to establish a joint venture, thus leading to the formation of Vistara, with Tata Sons holding a 51 per cent stake and Singapore Airlines owning 49 per cent.

Vistara took to the skies on 9 January 2015, with its inaugural flight from Delhi to Mumbai. The airline quickly gained a reputation for premium service at competitive rates. Within a few years, Vistara expanded its operations, launching its first international flight from Delhi to Singapore in August 2019.

2. Tata Teleservices

In the early 1990s, as India's economic landscape underwent a dramatic transformation, Ratan Tata spearheaded the formation of Tata Teleservices in a partnership with Bell Canada. The inception of Tata Teleservices was a direct response to the government's decision to open up the telecommunications sector to private players. Ratan Tata, ever the visionary, saw this as a chance to get ahead of the curve in terms of technology and service quality.

The decision to partner with Bell Canada was well-calculated due to the company's extensive experience in the North American telecommunications market. The company brought invaluable technological expertise and operational know-how to the table, which enabled Tata to leverage Bell Canada's existent capabilities. The partnership structure was carefully designed to ensure mutual benefit. While the exact equity distribution was not publicly disclosed, industry insiders suggested that Tata held a majority stake with Bell Canada as a significant minority partner. This arrangement allowed Tata to maintain control over the company's future direction.

The early years of Tata Teleservices were marred with complications. The Indian telecommunications landscape was still in its infancy, and the infrastructure was limited within a complex regulatory environment. Although Ratan acknowledged these hurdles, he also knew that the potential rewards were immense. Therefore, to manifest his vision, he adopted a multi-pronged strategy. Significant investments were made to construct a robust telecommunications network. This included setting up transmission towers, laying fibre-optic cables and establishing state-of-the-art switching centres.

Additionally, making use of Bell Canada's expertise, Tata Teleservices implemented cutting-edge technologies, including code division multiple access, for its mobile services. Next, to address the need for skilled professionals, the company invested heavily in training programmes and recruited top talent from both India and abroad and adopted a customer-centric approach from the outset, a trait that would become its hallmark in the years to come.

Although Tata Teleservices initially provided basic telephony services alone, including fixed-line connections and public call offices (PCOs), the company's service offerings began expanding with the evolving market. Thus, by the mid-1990s, Tata Teleservices had expanded into providing mobile telephony, internet services and enterprise solutions. Moreover, Ratan saw the scope of expansion in metropolitan areas and began targeting corporate clients and high-end individual consumers with premium services provided through leading-edge technology. To harness the vast untapped potential in rural

India, Ratan also invested in expanding the company's network to small towns and villages, thus often being the first to provide telecommunications services in these underserved areas.

The entry of Tata Teleservices had a dramatic impact on India's telecommunications sector as telephone density began to increase along with decreasing communication costs. Under Ratan Tata's leadership, the company deftly became, over time, one of India's largest telecom service providers.

Bell Canada office in Ottawa, Canada

Ratan Tata: His Life and Work I

28 December 1937	Ratan Tata is born in Mumbai (then Bombay) to Naval and Soonoo Tata. Naval Tata had been adopted by Ratanji Tata, the son of Jamsetji Tata, the founder of the Tata Group.
1955	Completes schooling at the Cathedral and John Connon School in Mumbai, followed by Bishop Cotton School in Shimla.
1962	Graduates with a degree in architecture from Cornell University, Ithaca, New York.
1962	Joins the Tata Group as an assistant in Tata Industries; spends six months training at the Jamshedpur plant of Tata Engineering and Locomotive Company, or Telco (now Tata Motors).
1963	Joins Tata Iron and Steel Company (TISCO) (now Tata Steel) at its Jamshedpur facility.
1965	Appointed as a technical officer in Tata Steel's engineering division.
1969	Works as the Tata Group's resident representative in Australia.
1970	Returns to India and briefly joins Tata Consultancy Services, which was then a fledgling software company.
1971	Becomes the director-in-charge of National Radio and Electronics (Nelco), a struggling electronics firm.
1974	Joins the board of Tata Sons as a director.
1975	Completes the Advanced Management Program at Harvard Business School.
1981	Is appointed chairman of Tata Industries, where he promotes high-technology businesses.
1986–1989	Serves as chairman of Air India, the national carrier.
25 March 1991	Takes over from J.R.D. Tata as chairman of Tata Sons and Tata Trusts; begins a clean-up exercise, driving out the satraps.
1991	Tata Motors forays into the passenger vehicle segment with the launch of the Tata Sierra.
1994	Tata Group exits edible oil and soap business; sells Tata Oil Mills (Tomco) to Hindustan Unilever.
1994	Titan enters the jewellery market with the launch of Tanishq.
1998	Tata Group sells Lakmé Cosmetics to Hindustan Unilever for ₹200 crore.
1998	Tata Motors launches Tata Indica, India's first indigenously designed and manufactured car, and Tata Safari, the country's first SUV.
1998	The group exits the pharma business; sells Merind, India's fourth-biggest pharma company, to Wockhardt for ₹95 crore.
1999	Tata Group exits Tata Information Systems Ltd (renamed Tata IBM), its 50:50 joint venture with IBM. It also sells its 10 per cent stake in IBM Global Services India.

Continued ...

3. Tata Petrodyne

One of the most ambitious ventures during India's early phase of economic liberalization was the establishment of Tata Petrodyne in 1993 through a collaboration with British Petroleum (BP). This partnership was made to capitalize on the Indian government's decision to open up the oil and gas sector to private and foreign investment. Ratan Tata thus decided to lead the Tata Group into a high-potential market that would also simultaneously address India's growing energy needs.

The partnership between Tata and BP was structured such that the strengths of both entities were leveraged. Ratan Tata brought to the table his deep understanding of the Indian market, strong governmental relationships built over years and a reputation for ethical business practices. BP contributed its vast technical expertise in oil and gas exploration along with cutting-edge technology and global industry experience. The equity structure of Tata Petrodyne reflected this balanced partnership, with Tata Industries holding a 51 per cent stake and BP owning the remaining 49 per cent – an arrangement that ensured Tata's control over the company's strategic direction.

Nonetheless, the upstream oil and gas sector presented numerous challenges for Tata Petrodyne. The industry was capital-intensive, technologically complex and subject to significant geological and market risks. Moreover, as a new entrant, Tata Petrodyne had to compete with established global players and state-owned enterprises, for which Ratan Tata came up with a multi-faceted strategy. Under his leadership, Tata Petrodyne invested in innovative exploration and production technologies such as seismic imaging techniques and novel oil recovery methods. The company also implemented comprehensive training programmes to produce highly skilled employees and often sent its Indian engineers to BP's global facilities for hands-on training and experience.

Considering the inherent uncertainties in oil and gas exploration, Tata Petrodyne developed robust risk assessment and management protocols by adopting several of BP's global best practices. Additionally, Tata Petrodyne adopted a selective approach to bidding for exploration blocks, focusing on areas with high potential but manageable risk profiles.

Tata Petrodyne's early years witnessed a series of significant operational milestones. In 1993, it secured its first exploration block in the Cambay Basin in Gujarat, marking its foray into active oil and gas exploration. By 1995, the company had expanded its operations to several offshore areas and was also conducting exploration activities in the Mumbai High region. Besides, Ratan Tata made skilful use of BP's global network by beginning to explore opportunities in Southeast Asia, particularly in Indonesia and Vietnam. By the subsequent year, Tata Petrodyne had established an advanced technology centre in Mumbai, where geophysical data analysis and reservoir modelling were prioritized.

The entry of Tata Petrodyne, along with other private players, impacted India's oil and gas sector in a major way by introducing competition, new and unprecedented technologies and fast-paced exploration ventures. Ratan Tata had foreseen that Tata Petrodyne would not only be profitable but would also contribute to India's energy security, which would solidify the trust of both consumers and the government in the Tata Group.

Despite its promising start, the late 1990s brought with them challenging issues for Tata Petrodyne in the form of fluctuating global oil prices, regulatory uncertainties and the inherent risks of exploration activities. To counter these hurdles, Ratan Tata employed the key strategy of portfolio diversification. While maintaining the company's focus on exploration and production, he ensured that Tata Petrodyne also ventured into related services like oilfield equipment manufacturing and technical consultancy. This approach was successfully able to mitigate risks and create additional revenue streams.

4. Tata Information Systems Limited

Staying true to his reputation of being ahead of his time, Ratan Tata identified the burgeoning prospects within the fast-growing information technology (IT) sector. In 1992, he spearheaded a groundbreaking partnership with IBM to launch Tata Information Systems Limited (TISL) as the Tata Group's formal entry into the IT domain. Ratan Tata rightly predicted that IT would be pivotal in enhancing operational efficiencies across various sectors and would enable Indian businesses to be part of a globalized economy. Therefore, he chose IBM for partnership owing to its reputation as one of the world's leading technology companies.

TISL was structured as a 50–50 joint venture between Tata Industries and IBM Corporation, and this equal partnership symbolized their mutual reverence and a shared vision. TISL's primary goal was to develop IT solutions tailored specifically to the Indian business landscape, as well as to address the unique challenges faced by Indian enterprises. The major challenges identified by Ratan Tata were limited access to technology, high IT-related costs and lack of technical expertise in the workforce. By providing affordable and scalable solutions, TISL aimed to democratize access to IT and empower businesses operating under various sectors. Hence, Ratan's vision for TISL included the introduction of advanced computing systems and software solutions; helping companies streamline processes, reduce costs and improve productivity through IT; enabling the development of local expertise; and creating a skilled workforce capable of implementing technological efficacy. Additionally, Ratan wanted TISL to cater to not only large corporations but also to small-to-medium enterprises.

With a comprehensive strategic framework to address India's IT needs, TISL quickly established itself as a pioneer in the country's IT scene by implementing several initiatives that had far-reaching impacts. The company was the first to develop industry-specific IT solutions for multiple sectors, including manufacturing, retail, banking and government services. Next, the company expanded its reach beyond metropolitan cities into smaller places like Pune, Coimbatore, Jamshedpur and Mysore – a move that was instrumental in introducing IT solutions to previously untapped markets. TISL also worked on making computing accessible to SMEs by offering much-needed solutions that were both efficient and cost-effective. As there was a considerable shortage of skilled IT professionals in India, TISL began several training programmes in collaboration with IBM's global teams that not only benefited Tata employees but also helped seed India's broader IT talent pool. Finally, TISL played an active role in enabling the country's digital transformation by providing data management systems and other IT services to the government.

Although it had a promising start with several successful milestones, in its early years, TISL had to deal with hurdles related to India's evolving regulatory environment that required constant adaptation, difficulty in convincing traditional and small businesses of the benefits of adopting IT solutions and the entry of other multinational players into India's IT sector. However, Ratan ensured that these problems were skilfully addressed through a customer-oriented approach that centred around client needs and tailored solutions. By the mid-1990s, TISL had firmly established itself as a leader in India's IT sector. Its success formed the basis of future ventures within the Tata Group, most notably Tata Consultancy Services (TCS), which would go on to become one of the world's largest IT service providers.

In 1997, TISL was renamed Tata IBM Ltd. However, by 1999, Tata had decided to exit the joint venture and retain only a symbolic 1 per cent stake while IBM took full control of operations under the name IBM India. Although short-lived as a partnership, TISL had the enduring impact of introducing global best practices in India and fostering technological innovation, which was largely responsible for India's growing reputation as an emerging IT hub.

Investments in Research and Development across Industries

Ratan Tata had immense belief in the importance of continuous research and development (R&D) to drive innovation and maintain a competitive edge. During his lifetime, he made significant investments in R&D across various industries, which effectively positioned the Tata Group at the forefront of technological advancement and innovation in India. Additionally, although many of the products and services below were launched after Ratan's retirement as chairman of Tata Sons in 2012, they were effectively an extension of his vision and values through his oversight as chairman emeritus.

The fruits of Ratan Tata's strategic investments in R&D are evident in the numerous 'firsts' achieved by Tata companies, the thousands of patents filed, and the recognition received globally. The Boston Consulting Group's ranking of the Tata Group as the only Indian enterprise on its list of 50 Most Innovative Companies in 2023 is a testament to the culmination of Ratan Tata's long-held vision.

The Automotive Sector

Ratan Tata single-handedly transformed Tata Motors into a powerhouse of automotive innovation. The company's R&D efforts under Ratan's supervision peaked in several groundbreaking achievements.

- **Tata Indica:** Launched in 1998, the Tata Indica was India's first indigenously designed and manufactured passenger car, which helped showcase the country's engineering capabilities.

- **Tata Nano:** Unveiled in 2008, the Tata Nano was conceptualized as the world's most affordable car. This ambitious project aimed to make car ownership accessible to millions of Indian families. The Nano's development required advanced engineering solutions to meet its price point while maintaining safety and quality standards.

- **Electric vehicles:** Under Ratan Tata, Tata Motors invested heavily in electric vehicle (EV) technology. These efforts led to the development of automobiles like the Nexon EV Max, which became the first EV to cross the world's highest motorable road – to Uming La Pass in Eastern Ladakh, which is 19,024 feet above sea level.

The company's commitment to R&D is evident in its patent filings. In FY2023 alone, Tata Motors filed a record 158 patents and 79 designs, the highest cumulative number for any Indian automotive manufacturer.

Steel Industry

Tata Steel, under Ratan Tata's guidance, continued its legacy of innovation that began with India's first industrial R&D division established in 1937. The company's R&D efforts in Ratan Tata's later years as chairman focused on sustainability and efficiency, particularly through the following programmes:

- **FerroHaat:** Launched in 2020, this global first-of-its-kind digital app provides an organized system for steel scrap sourcing.

- **Tata Aggreto and Tata Nirman:** These are India's first branded steel slag products, demonstrating Tata Steel's ability to create value from waste.

- **Green Steel:** Tata Steel's R&D efforts included developing more environment-friendly steel production methods that align with global sustainability goals.

Information Technology

- **Tata Consultancy Services (TCS):** Under Ratan Tata's leadership, TCS emerged as a global IT powerhouse with its R&D initiatives being at the forefront of India's digital transformation.

TCS stall, India Mobile Congress 2022 Exhibition, Pragati Maidan , New Delhi

- **Tata Research Development and Design Centre:** Established in 1981, this was India's first dedicated software R&D centre. It has been instrumental in developing cutting-edge software solutions and driving innovation in the IT sector.

- **Supercomputing:** In 2007, TCS developed a supercomputer called Eka, which was the fastest in Asia then.

- **Digital governance:** TCS's R&D efforts led to the transformation of India's Passport Seva Kendra in 2008, showing the potential of technology in improving public services.

Consumer Products

Ratan Tata wanted consumer products to also be considered when working on new ideas, especially considering the unique needs of the Indian market.

- **Tata Salt:** Launched in 1983, Tata Salt was India's first branded iodized salt launched to address a significant public health concern.

- **Tata Tea:** In 1985, Tata Tea introduced the poly pack format, reimagining the packaged tea market in India.

Recent R&D efforts at Tata Consumer Products have prioritized health and wellness products. For instance, the company launched Tata Salt Iron Health, a category-first iodized salt with added iron. The company's R&D expenditure in FY2022–23 alone was a whopping ₹36.35 crore.

Telecommunications

We have already read about how, recognizing the potential of the telecommunications sector, Ratan Tata led the formation of Tata Teleservices in partnership with Bell Canada in 1992. This venture focused on developing telecommunications infrastructure and services tailored to the Indian market. The company invested heavily in building a robust network, including transmission towers, fibre-optic cables and highly advanced switching centres.

Energy and Power

Under Ratan Tata's leadership, the group made the following significant strides in energy and power sector innovation:

Tata Power: The company has been at the forefront of developing smart energy solutions. In 2021, Tata Power deployed India's first smart meters featuring NB-IoT communications, marking a significant step towards updating India's power infrastructure.

Tata Chemicals: The company commissioned the first carbon capture unit in the United Kingdom, proving the group's commitment to addressing climate change through technological innovation.

Aerospace and Defence

Ratan Tata's vision extended to the aerospace and defence sectors. Tata Advanced Systems, started in 2007, is a company that offers end-to-end innovative solutions to the aerospace and defence sectors. It has entered into partnerships and joint ventures with leading aerospace and defence firms across the world. Its design and full platform assembly services cover areas as wide as satellites, missiles, radars, unmanned aerial systems, artillery guns, command and control systems, optronics, homeland security and land systems. It also offers services for aircraft and helicopters.

In 2021, Tata Advanced Systems began to set up final assembly line, the first of its kind in India, for the Airbus C295 at Vadodra, Gujarat. The main purpose of the facility is to provide support to the Indian Air Force with indigenous manufacturing under the Government of India's 'AatmaNirbhar Bharat' (Self-reliant India) programme. The facility was inaugurated in October 2024, and the first indigenously made C295 is scheduled to roll out in September 2026. Under the C295 deal they have signed, Tata Advanced Systems will provide forty C295 aircraft to the Indian Air Force; they will procure another sixteen from Spain.

Cross-Industry Innovation Initiatives

Tata InnoVista: This annual innovation event, initiated under Ratan Tata's leadership, has grown significantly. In 2022, it drew over 36,000 innovators from thirty-eight Tata companies, who participated with more than 15,000 innovations.

Academic partnerships: Tata companies have actively collaborated with academic institutions to drive innovation. For instance, Tata Consumer Products has partnered with various research institutes, including the Council of Scientific Research labs, to develop new technologies and products.

Future-Focused Investments

Tata Electronics: This venture, started in continuation of Ratan Tata's vision after his retirement, aims to enter the semiconductor production space, which is a critical area for India's technological independence. India's first commercial semiconductor plant – the first fabrication lab, called fab – is being constructed at Dholera, Gujarat. The decision to enter the semiconductor industry in a joint venture with Taiwan's Powerchip Semiconductor Manufacturing Corporation (PSMC) was announced by N. Chandrasekaran, the current chairman of Tata Sons, in January 2024. The first fab under this plan will be able to produce 50,000 wafers – thin slices of semiconductors – each month (at full capacity). The semiconductor chips produced here will be used widely in automotive, data storage, wireless communication and artificial intelligence (AI) sectors.

Tata Electronics Private Limited (TEPL) has a target of employing women to cover eighty-five per cent of its workforce at its manufacturing facility located in the Krishnagiri district of Tamil Nadu.

Agratas Energy Storage Solutions: This initiative focuses on battery manufacturing, thus positioning the group in the rapidly growing energy storage sector.

CHAPTER 4

MAJOR MILESTONES AND ICONIC PROJECTS

- Landmark Acquisitions
- The Tata Nano Project
- Tata Consultancy Services (TCS) and Technological Ventures

Ratan Tata's tenure as chairman of the Tata Group from 1991 to 2012 was a largely transformative period that propelled the conglomerate onto the global stage. Due to some groundbreaking projects initiated under his guidance, the group's revenue grew over forty times, from $4 billion to $100 billion, with the profit increase of more than fifty times.

The era of Ratan Tata's chairmanship was characterised by a series of iconic projects and acquisitions. The purchase of Tetley, Corus and Jaguar Land Rover stands out as testament to his ambition and business foresight. In the domestic market, Ratan Tata spearheaded projects that captured the nation's imagination. In particular, the launch of the Tata Indica in 1998 was a watershed moment in the history of India's automotive industry. This was followed by the ambitious Tata Nano project in 2008, which aimed to make car ownership accessible to

In October 1997, the Tata Group was rocked by what came to be known as the 'Tata Tapes' controversy. This scandal erupted when journalist Ritu Sarin of the *Indian Express* published transcripts of telephonic conversations involving Nusli Wadia, a prominent industrialist, and several high-profile figures, including Ratan Tata. The tapes revealed discussions about Tata Tea's ongoing problems with the Assam government, which had accused the company of having connections with the United Liberation Front of Assam (ULFA), a banned separatist organisation. The secretly taped conversations suggested that the Tatas were attempting to secure central government intervention in their dispute with the Assam authorities. This controversy unfolded against a backdrop of allegations by Prafulla Kumar Mahanta, then chief minister of Assam, accusing the Tatas of anti-national conduct. The situation escalated when Assam police interrogated and arrested Tata Tea executives on charges of aiding ULFA activities. The release of these recorded conversations sparked intense debate regarding ethical standards in corporate practices, the extent of political influence wielded by businesses and the appropriate limits of interaction between private enterprises and governmental bodies. It also sparked a debate on privacy and the legality of phone tapping. Federal authorities refuted any connection to the wiretapping incident, while the home secretary called for a thorough investigation into what appeared to be unlawful monitoring activities. The company continues to maintain its innocence in the scandal, asserting that any financial assistance provided was part of a medical aid scheme for the Assamese people. The Tata Tapes controversy highlighted the importance of transparency in corporations' dealings with government bodies. For Ratan Tata, the scandal was a test in crisis management that required him to balance the protection of corporate interests with maintaining public trust. This incident also illuminated the glaring need and lack of clear guidelines in corporate–government interactions

Ratan Tata Quotes

Take the stones people throw at you, and use them to build a monument.

millions of Indians. Moreover, under Ratan Tata's oversight, Tata Consultancy Services (TCS) emerged as a global IT powerhouse, with its public listing in 2004 being India's first $1 billion IPO by a private-sector company.

Landmark Acquisitions

The Tata Group gained a formidable reputation in the Indian business scene thanks to three major global acquisitions under Ratan Tata's chairmanship.

Tetley Tea

1. Tetley Tea

The acquisition of Tetley Tea – which was founded in 1837 by the Tetley brothers from Yorkshire, England – by Tata Tea in 2000 was a landmark deal valued at £271 million (approximately $432 million). It was the largest cross-border acquisition by an Indian company at the time. Tetley was a much-loved British tea brand that made a significant impact on the tea industry by pioneering the widespread use of tea bags. This groundbreaking innovation transformed the way people consumed tea, offering a more efficient and user-friendly method of preparation. The introduction of tea bags proved to be a game-changer for Tetley, contributing substantially to its growth in an era when consumers increasingly opted for convenience.

The journey towards this historic acquisition began in the early 1990s when R.K. Krishna Kumar, then managing director of Tata Tea, recognized the potential for the Group's international expansion following the fall of the Berlin Wall. This geopolitical shift signalled new opportunities, prompting Kumar and Ratan to consider strategic moves that would position Tata Tea as a global player. In 1994, Ratan Tata made his first attempt to acquire Tetley by dispatching a carefully assembled team to London; this initial effort was unsuccessful due to financing challenges. Thereafter, Tetley was acquired by a private equity firm.

However, fate intervened in 1999 when Tetley's new owners put the company back on the market. This time, Ratan Tata was prepared. In June 1999, in the boardroom at Bombay House (head office of the Tata Group), the Tata Tea board of directors, chaired by Ratan Tata, gave the go-ahead for the acquisition. This decision was made based on a clear strategic rationale – to capitalise on potential synergies in tea sourcing, supply chain and new geographical markets by acquiring a world-renowned tea brand.

The Tetley acquisition was ingenious not only in its scale but also in its financial structure. It was the first leveraged buyout successfully executed by an Indian company, and it allowed Tata Tea to minimise its cash outlay while retaining 100 per cent ownership of Tetley. The purchase was funded through a combination of equity subscribed by Tata Tea, junior loan stock from institutional investors and senior debt facilities arranged by Rabobank International. This financial structure enabled Tata Tea, with a net worth of only $114 million, to acquire a company valued at $450 million – more than four times its size.

The acquisition of Tetley transformed and catapulted Tata Tea to become the second-largest tea company worldwide, behind only Unilever. This strategic move provided Tata Tea with several key advantages. Tetley was a well-established brand with a strong presence in the markets of the United Kingdom, Canada and the United States, among other countries. After the acquisition, Tetley became the number one tea brand in the United Kingdom by volume and number two by value. The deal provided the Tata Group with access to new markets for expansion, particularly France, Poland and Australia. The combined entity could now acquire tea globally from low-cost sources, successfully offsetting the challenges faced by the Indian tea industry. Moreover, Tata Tea was able to gain access to Tetley's renowned blending skills, which greatly enhanced its product quality and performance consistency.

The Tetley acquisition had a profound impact on the Indian tea market. It heralded a new era of confidence in Indian corporate governance and the ability of Indian companies to compete globally. Additionally, it set a precedent for other Indian enterprises that aspired to operate internationally, paving the way for even more cross-border acquisitions by Indian businesses.

Despite the acquisition's strategic importance, the market initially perceived it negatively for about three years due to the high debt burden and integration challenges. However, over time, Ratan Tata's vision of transforming Tata Tea into a global beverage company became realized, which vindicated his bold move. The major challenges faced by Tata Tea in the post-acquisition phase included cultural differences between tea consumers from India and abroad, the cyclical downturn in the tea industry and increased competition from substitute products. Nonetheless, the Tata Group adopted a patient and strategic approach to integration with a considerable focus on exploring synergies without time pressures and maintaining operational independence. They emphasized revenue growth rather than cost reduction, allowing for a smoother transition. Soon after the acquisition, Tetley was able to bring down its debt-equity ratio from 3:1 to 1.75:1 within two years through prudent financial management. Over time, synergies were achieved in tea sourcing and a significant amount of profit began to be generated in the East European and Middle Eastern markets.

2. Daewoo Commercial Vehicles

One of the most significant milestones of the Tata Group under the leadership of Ratan Tata was Tata Motors' acquisition of Daewoo Commercial Vehicle Company (DWCV) in 2004. During this period, Tata Motors was already India's largest truck manufacturer but lacked a strong presence in the heavy commercial vehicle segment, especially in international markets, and was actively seeking opportunities to expand its global portfolio.

Daewoo Commercial Vehicle Company, a part of the larger Daewoo Group, had fallen into financial difficulties following the Asian fiscal crisis of the late 1990s. Despite its monetary troubles, DWCV was known for its high-quality heavy trucks and had a significant market share in South Korea, which presented an ideal opportunity for Tata Motors to enter the East Asian market and acquire valuable technology and expertise in heavy commercial vehicles.

On 18 February 2004, Tata Motors signed an investment agreement to acquire Daewoo Commercial Vehicle for $102 million. The deal structure was innovative – Tata Motors would pay $51 million upfront, while the remaining $51 million would be raised by DWCV through loans from South Korean institutions. The acquisition was completed on 29 March 2004, with Ratan Tata personally attending the ceremony in Gunsan, South Korea.

This event marked the largest Indian acquisition in South Korea at the time.

DWCV was the second-largest manufacturer of heavy trucks in South Korea, with a 25 per cent market share, which immediately gave Tata Motors a strong presence in the heavy commercial vehicle segment. The acquisition provided Tata Motors with a foothold in the South Korean market and a platform to expand into other East Asian markets. Tata Motors gained perpetual and exclusive rights to use Daewoo trademarks in Korea and other overseas markets for DWCV's product range.

The combined strengths of Tata Motors and DWCV led to the development of new products. Ravi Kant, executive director of Tata Motors, mentioned plans for creating the 'truck of the future' with a prototype expected by 2005–06. The acquisition enhanced Tata Motors' reputation as a global player in the commercial vehicle sector and demonstrated its ability to manage and integrate international operations. After the acquisition, DWCV was renamed Tata Daewoo Commercial Vehicle (TDCV). It proved to be a successful venture for Tata Motors.

3. NatSteel

Tata Steel's acquisition of NatSteel in 2004 was a bid to expand Tata Steel's manufacturing footprint across seven new countries in Asia. However, it also had the additional effect of propelling the company's global ranking in the steel industry from the 56th to 28th position.

In the early 2000s, Ratan Tata was actively pursuing global expansion opportunities for the Tata Group. In particular, Tata Steel, as one of the group's flagship companies, was looking to extend its reach beyond India's borders. The company's management, led by B. Muthuraman, identified NatSteel as an attractive acquisition target for several reasons. NatSteel was Singapore's largest steel company, which had a strong presence in Southeast and East Asia – regions where Tata Steel had limited exposure. The company owned steel mills in China, Thailand, Vietnam, the Philippines and Australia, and primarily manufactured long products such as rebars, wire rods and pre-stressed concrete wires and strands. This portfolio significantly expanded Tata Steel's existing product range and offered a gateway into high-growth markets like China.

On 16 August 2004, Tata Steel signed a definitive share subscription agreement with NatSteel to acquire its steel businesses in an all-cash deal. The transaction was structured such that NatSteel would spin off its entire steel business into a wholly owned subsidiary called NatSteel Asia Pvt Ltd, after which Tata Steel would acquire 100 per cent of the equity capital of NatSteel Asia. The enterprise value of the acquisition was set at S$486.4 million (approximately ₹1,313 crore at the time), including the equity value of NatSteel Asia, its debt and working capital requirements. The deal was considered cost-effective compared to setting up a new integrated steel plant of similar capacity, with the per-tonne acquisition cost estimated at around Rs 6,000, significantly lower than the ₹17,000 per tonne for Tata Steel's expansion plans.

The acquisition process took several months to complete due to the need for regulatory approvals across multiple jurisdictions. On 16 February 2005, Tata Steel announced the successful completion of the acquisition in a deal in which all of NatSteel's steel assets in Singapore, Malaysia, Thailand, Vietnam, Philippines, Australia and two out of three companies in China were transferred to NatSteel Asia. A notable exception to the transfer was the Changzhou Wujin NatSteel Company in China, which was delayed due to pending regulatory approvals. To address this hiccup, Tata Steel signed a supplemental subscription agreement with NatSteel, paying S$304.8 million initially, with the remaining S$60 million to be paid once the Chinese steel company became part of NatSteel Asia.

The acquisition of NatSteel provided Tata Steel with several strategic advantages. With increased production capacity, Tata Steel's consolidated capacity rose from four million tonnes per annum to six million tonnes, with the potential to reach seven million tonnes after completing ongoing expansion in Jamshedpur. NatSteel's focus on producing long products also complemented Tata Steel's existing production portfolio, allowing for a more diversified offering. The acquisition created opportunities for increased cost efficiency in raw material sourcing. As a result, Tata Steel began supplying semi-finished steel and billets to NatSteel's manufacturing facilities, replacing their reliance on scrap.

The deal increased Tata Steel's manufacturing presence to seven new countries in Asia, thereby considerably enhancing its global footprint. The market impact of the acquisition was monumental. The deal was India's second-largest overseas acquisition in 2004, which symbolized the country's emergence as a source of foreign direct investment.

Internationally, the acquisition garnered acclaim and respect for Tata Steel. It showcased the company's financial and strategic potentiality resulting in Indian companies playing an increasingly prominent role in the global steel industry.

Despite the strategic benefits, the acquisition presented challenges for Tata Steel that were handled deftly by Ratan Tata. Managing a cross-border acquisition of this scale required careful integration of different corporate cultures and practices. Additionally, the cyclical nature of the steel industry and potential volatility in Asian markets posed several risks to the investment's success. However, Ratan Tata saw these challenges as opportunities for further expansion in Asia, which set the stage for even larger acquisitions in the future, such as the Corus Group in 2007.

4. Corus Steel

The acquisition of Corus Group plc., by Tata Steel in 2007 was one of the largest overseas acquisitions by an Indian company at the time. This move spearheaded by Ratan Tata elevated Tata Steel from a mere regional player into the fifth-largest steel producer in the world.

In 2006, Tata Steel's production capacity was insufficient to rank among the top 50 steel companies worldwide. Recognizing the need for rapid expansion to compete on the world stage, Ratan Tata and his team set their sights on Corus, which was Europe's second-largest steel producer. The rationale behind this decision was that Corus offered a strong distribution network in Europe, expertise in high-end steel production for automotive and aerospace industries, and the potential for significant synergies with Tata Steel's low-cost manufacturing base in India.

The acquisition process was far from straightforward. What began as a friendly takeover soon turned into a fierce bidding war with Brazil's Companhia Siderúrgica Nacional (CSN). The initial offer from Tata Steel in October 2006 was 455 pence per share, which valued Corus at £4.3 billion. However, CSN's entry into the bid in December 2006 triggered a protracted battle that would last until 31 January 2007.

The climax of this corporate drama unfolded in a nine-round auction orchestrated by the UK Takeover Panel. In a nail-biting finish, Tata Steel emerged victorious with a final bid of 608 pence per share, narrowly edging out CSN's 603 pence. This final offer valued Corus at £6.2 billion (US$12 billion), which represented a premium of 68 per cent over Corus's average share price for the preceding 12 months.

The acquisition of Corus aligned perfectly with Tata Steel's strategic vision. It provided instant access to European markets, a more sophisticated customer base, and exposure to high-growth sectors like automotive and construction industries. The combined entity boasted an annual crude steel production capacity of 27 million tonnes with a large number of employees – 84,000 across four continents. This was because Tata Steel's expertise in low-cost manufacturing complemented Corus's high-end processing facilities in Europe. Moreover, the deal facilitated cross-fertilization of R&D capabilities, particularly in packaging and construction.

The acquisition sent major shockwaves through the worldwide steel industry as it signalled the competency of Indian companies to participate in the international scene. It also resulted in challenging the traditional dominance of Western and Japanese steel giants of the time, and the deal was celebrated in India due to its contribution to the country's growing economic clout.

Financially, the all-cash deal was a significant undertaking for Tata Steel, and several analysts and detractors voiced their concern about the risk owing to the high price paid, especially considering Corus's declining profitability in 2006. Tata Steel had to raise substantial debt to finance the acquisition, leading to some analysts worrying about the financial burden. There were further concerns about the integration challenges given the vast difference in size between the two companies – Corus being nearly four times larger than Tata Steel in terms of revenue. The acquisition was also poorly timed, completed just before the 2008 global financial crisis, which severely impacted steel demand. Moreover, Ratan Tata underestimated the structural challenges facing UK steel, including high energy costs and raw material security issues. The subsequent downturn in the global steel market put significant pressure on the combined entity's finances, and this acquisition soon became a cautionary tale of corporate overreach. The debt burden from the deal proved challenging, and Corus's underperforming UK assets became a significant liability, with Tata Steel UK reportedly losing $1 million a day by 2016. Despite attempts at restructuring, including idling blast furnaces, cutting jobs and selling assets, the European operations continued to struggle financially.

Tata Steel plant at Port Talbot, South Wales, UK

In 2010, Tata rebranded Corus Steel as Tata Steel Europe, but by 2016 Tata Steel acknowledged its mistake. Twelve years after the acquisition, Tata Steel was considering selling its UK assets. The UK's Brexit vote further complicated matters. A proposed merger with ThyssenKrupp, intended to consolidate European steel operations, was agreed upon in 2017 but ultimately blocked by the European Commission in 2019 due to antitrust concerns. This setback prompted a shift towards independent restructuring and a strong emphasis on decarbonisation. Tata Steel began operating with more distinct focuses on its UK and Netherlands divisions, culminating in the establishment of Tata Steel UK and Tata Steel Netherlands in 2021.

The British Labour government inked a deal in September 2024 with Tata Steel that will provide £500m subsidy to the company. This grant is aimed at building a new electric arc furnace at the Port Talbot steelworks in Wales. While this is an opportunity for the employees to scale up their efficiency, with training and other support, this also paves the way to the loss of more than 2,500 jobs on grounds of redundancy as Tata has shut down one of its two blast furnaces in Port Talbot.

Jaguar Land Rover

Jaguar Land Rover (JLR) was acquired by Tata Motors in 2008 in a $2.3 billion all-cash deal. The journey towards acquiring JLR began with Ford Motor Company's decision to divest its luxury car brands. Ford had earlier purchased Jaguar for $2.5 billion in 1989 and Land Rover for $2.7 billion in 2000. However, by the mid-2000s, Ford was struggling to derive the desired profits from these brands. JLR was facing significant market setbacks due to its outdated retro design and inefficient engines at a time when fuel prices were soaring continually. These factors, combined with the global financial crisis at the time, led Ford to decide to sell these iconic British cars.

Tata Motors, under Ratan Tata's guidance, saw this as an excellent opportunity to enter the high-end premier automobile market internationally. The company's long-term strategy included consolidating its position in the domestic Indian market while expanding worldwide through acquisitions and strategic collaborations.

Therefore, in March 2008, Ford announced the sale of Jaguar and Land Rover to the Tata Group. The deal was finalized on 2 June 2008, with Tata Motors purchasing JLR for $2.3 billion on a cash-free, debt-free basis. This purchase price was close to half of what Ford had originally paid for both brands. The acquisition also included JLR's manufacturing plants, two advanced design centres in the United Kingdom, country-specific sales companies

Jaguar XJ

Land Rover Defender

spanning the world, and, finally, licences for all necessary intellectual property rights. Furthermore, Ford agreed to contribute up to $600 million to JLR's pension funds as part of the deal.

Ratan Tata's rationale behind this acquisition was multifaceted. First, it would help Tata Motors acquire a global footprint and enter the luxury automobile market. Second, through this deal, Tata gained access to two advanced design studios as well as Ford's technological expertise, which would allow the former to improve their core products in India. Lastly, there was a potential cost advantage as Tata's recently acquired Corus Steel was the main supplier of automotive high-grade steel to JLR and other automobile manufacturers in the American and European markets.

Since the acquisition happened during a global financial crisis, in the 10 months after the acquisition, JLR's sales plunged 32 per cent, and the unit recorded a loss of £281 million. Tata Motors' total debt in March 2009 increased to ₹43,580 crore – nearly double of what it owed in the previous fiscal year. Nonetheless, Ratan Tata countered these problems by implementing a three-point strategy focusing on improving liquidity, cost control and new product development. Following the purchase, Tata Motors began investing significant amounts in automotive research and development, which helped revitalize the Jaguar and Land Rover brands. The results of these efforts became apparent soon, when in 2011, JLR's sales surged to £9.87 billion, and by 2018, they more than doubled their sales to over £25 billion. Consequently, in the fiscal year 2024, JLR reported sales of over 4,00,000 vehicles, thereby helping Tata Motors evolve into a formidable international player. The company now boasted ownership of both the world's cheapest car, the Nano, and luxury marques such as Jaguar and Land Rover.

The acquisition significantly enhanced Tata Motors' international presence and brand value. Customers' perception of Jaguar and Land Rover improved markedly in the post-acquisition years, and the brands were no longer seen as struggling. In India, the acquisition was hailed as the country's 'Neil Armstrong moment' – signifying 'a single step for Tata but a giant leap for India'. It demonstrated the capability of Indian companies to manage and revive international brands, boosting confidence in India's corporate sector. The deal also opened up opportunities for Tata Motors to introduce luxury vehicles to the Indian market as the country's economy and disposable incomes increased.

Over time, the acquisition proved to be a sound financial decision for Ratan Tata to the significant growth of JLR's contribution to Tata Motors' revenue. By 2014, eighty-three per cent of Tata

Motors' total revenue and 90 per cent of the net profit came from Jaguar Land Rover. Moreover, the valuation of JLR soared from the initial $2.3 billion acquisition price to $14 billion in just five years, thus becoming one of the most important examples of Ratan Tata's business acumen and foresight.

The Tata Nano Project

The Tata Nano, often hailed as the 'people's car', was an ambitious project undertaken by Ratan Tata that aimed to revolutionize the automotive market in India. The genesis of this car can be traced back to a poignant observation made by Ratan Tata. As he recounted in a heartfelt Instagram post years after the Nano's

Tata Nano

In 2006, Tata chose Singur, a small town in West Bengal, as the site for the ambitious Nano project. However, this area's allocation to his project soon spiralled into one of the most contentious chapters in the Tata Group's history. The site for setting up the Nano factory was originally farmland, and its selection by Tata Motors was met with widespread discontent and opposition from displaced farmers even as bulldozers rolled into Singur's lush grounds. The farmers were afraid of losing their livelihoods, and they found champion of their cause in Mamata Banerjee, who was then the opposition leader in the state. Things became worse when, at a press conference, Ratan Tata delivered a statement saying that he would not pull out of Singur even at gunpoint. However, his metaphorical trigger was pulled when he announced the project's relocation to Gujarat in October 2008. The legal battle over the Singur controversy was a protracted affair that unfolded over several years, culminating in a landmark Supreme Court judgement on 31 August 2016. Initially, the Calcutta High Court had upheld the land acquisition for the Tata Nano project in 2007. However, the Supreme Court's verdict quashed the West Bengal government's acquisition of 997 acres of agricultural land and ordering its return to the 9,117 landowners. The court declared the acquisition to be 'illegal' and not for public purpose, directing the land's return within 12 weeks while allowing farmers to retain their compensation. The legal saga continued with Tata Motors initiating arbitration proceedings against the West Bengal Industrial Development Corporation (WBIDC), and on 30 October 2023, an arbitral tribunal ruled in favour of Tata Motors by awarding the company ₹766 crore with 11 per cent interest per annum along with ₹1 crore in legal charges. Nonetheless, the Singur controversy cast a long shadow over Ratan Tata's reputation despite the majority of blame lying with the West Bengal state government. The project's potential displacement of farmers and degradation of fertile land led to charges of insensitivity towards low-income agricultural communities and the secrecy surrounding the deal between Tata Motors and the government fuelled accusations of a lack of transparency. Questions were raised about allowing the acquisition of the land in the first place under the colonial-era Land Acquisition Act. An open letter penned by Ratan Tata, which asked people to choose between industrial growth and a 'destructive political environment', was perceived as confrontational and dishonest. In later years, Ratan Tata's expression of deep affection for the Singur project and regret over its failure revealed the emotional toll of the controversy on him.

launch, the inspiration struck when he constantly witnessed Indian families precariously balanced on scooters, often with a child sandwiched between the parents, navigating slippery roads. This sight moved him deeply, igniting a desire to create a safer and more comfortable alternative.

Initially, Ratan Tata and his team had explored ways to enhance the safety of two-wheelers. However, Ratan's background in architecture and his penchant for sketching led him to envision something more ambitious. What began as a doodle of a basic dune buggy without windows or doors eventually evolved into the concept of a four-wheeled vehicle that would be both safe and affordable.

The journey from concept to reality for the Tata Nano required addressing several challenges, mostly related to cost reduction. Ratan Tata set an audacious goal for his team – to create a car that would retail for just ₹1 lakh (approximately $2,500 at the time). This price point was revolutionary as it aimed to bridge the gap between two-wheelers and entry-level cars, making four-wheeler ownership a reality for millions of Indians. To achieve this ambitious target, the Tata Motors team had to rethink every aspect of automotive design and manufacturing. The development process was characterised by relentless cost-cutting measures and innovative engineering solutions. The initial design of the Nano included many non-essential features. Moreover, it featured only a driver's side wing mirror, one wiper blade and three lug nuts per wheel instead of the standard four. The Nano was the first car to utilize a 2-cylinder petrol engine with a single balancer shaft in a bid to prioritize efficiency and cost-effectiveness. Additionally, the team focused on reducing the amount of steel used in the car's construction without compromising safety.

To keep costs down, Tata Motors emphasized sourcing components locally. The Nano boasted over 95 per cent local content from its launch, a feat that required close collaboration with suppliers. Furthermore, instead of annual contracts, Tata Motors established long-term volume contracts with suppliers, which contributed to driving down its costs considerably.

The unveiling of the Tata Nano at the 2008 Auto Expo in New Delhi was a momentous occasion. Marketed as India's first 'one lakh rupee car,' the Nano sparked widespread curiosity and excitement. The promise of an affordable and safer alternative to two-wheelers resonated with millions of Indian families, and the initial response was downright overwhelming. When bookings opened, Tata Motors received 2,06,000 orders, far exceeding their production capacity at the time. However, despite the initial enthusiasm, the road to mass production for the Nano was problematic. One of the most significant setbacks occurred early in the production phase. The original manufacturing plant for the Nano was planned in Singur, West Bengal. However, political opposition and protests over land acquisition forced Tata Motors to relocate the entire production facility to Sanand, Gujarat, resulting in significant delays and increased costs, which complicated the ambitious pricing strategy central to the car's appeal.

When the Nano hit the roads, it faced several more unforeseen problems that impacted its market performance. Early incidents of Nano cars catching fire raised concerns about the vehicle's safety, despite Tata Motors' assurances and investigations. Moreover, the aggressive cost-cutting measures, while necessary to meet the price target, led to perceptions of the Nano as a 'cheap' car rather than an affordable one. The car's marketing strategy labelling it the 'cheapest car' alienated the brand-conscious Indian middle class. Thus, the initial distribution strategy failed to effectively reach the target consumer segment, particularly in rural and semi-urban areas. Also, many potential buyers in the target customer base faced difficulties in securing financing for the Nano, severely limiting its accessibility.

These factors contributed to sales figures that fell far short of the initial projections. Although Tata Motors had anticipated annual sales of 2,50,000 units, the actual numbers were significantly lower. By the 2016–2017 model year, sales had dwindled to just 7,591 units.

In response to these challenges, Tata Motors implemented several strategies to rejuvenate the Nano. The company shifted its marketing focus from price to value, emphasizing the Nano's features and benefits. The subsequent iterations of the Nano included enhanced features and improvements based on customer feedback. Tata Motors set up smaller, more accessible showrooms to reach a broader customer base, particularly in semi-urban and rural areas. The company also worked on partnerships with financial institutions to make car loans more accessible to potential Nano buyers.

Ultimately, the production of the Tata Nano ceased in 2018 due to a confluence of factors. Primarily, the car failed to meet the new safety and emissions standards implemented in India. The necessity for anti-lock braking systems and updated crash test norms made its upgrading financially unfeasible for Tata Motors. Further, poor sales figures significantly contributed to the decision to halt production; in 2018, only one Nano was assembled, compared to 275 in the previous year. The initial promise of a ₹1,00,000 ($2,200) price tag could not be maintained, with the final, safer product costing significantly more, effectively making the Nano commercially unviable.

Ratan Tata, known for his candour and willingness to learn from setbacks, openly acknowledged the challenges he had faced during the Nano project. He attributed much of the Nano's struggle to marketing missteps, particularly the emphasis he had placed on its low price rather than its value proposition. In hindsight, Tata noted that the average age of the Nano's design team was just 25 to 26, highlighting the enthusiasm and fresh perspective that went into creating an affordable vehicle. However, he felt that the sales team mismanaged the branding by promoting the Nano as the 'cheapest car' instead of positioning it as an accessible vehicle for the average Indian family.

While the Tata Nano may not have achieved the commercial success that was initially envisioned by Ratan Tata, its impact on the Indian automotive industry was undeniable. The Nano project pushed the boundaries of frugal engineering and cost-effective manufacturing, a factor that contributed significantly to the creation of a new segment of ultra-affordable vehicles by competitors. The Nano's production and distribution had also created new entrepreneurial opportunities across India, particularly in the supply chain and dealership networks. The car also garnered international attention due to its demonstration of India's engineering capabilities. The anticipation and introduction of the Nano had a surprising impact on the used car market in India, as many potential buyers reconsidered their choices to purchase second-hand cars when they could buy a new car in a similar price. The Nano project also spurred research into alternative fuel technologies, including compressed air and electric versions (E-Nano), thereby aligning it with growing environmental concerns.

The story of the Tata Nano provides an interesting insight into Ratan Tata's legendary vision, innovative prescience and the idea behind bringing a revolutionary product to market. Although his dream of making car ownership a reality for every Indian family might not have been fully realized in the way he initially envisioned, it demonstrated his commitment to social responsibility. It successfully challenged conventional wisdom in the automobile industry and sparked important conversations about affordability, safety and accessibility in personal transportation. The lessons learnt from this ambitious project have informed subsequent endeavours by Tata Motors and other manufacturers, particularly in developing markets in which the need for affordable, safe transportation remains pressing.

Tata Consultancy Services and Technological Ventures

Tata Consultancy Services (TCS) has been a crown jewel in the Tata Group's portfolio, with its roots tracing back to J.R.D. Tata and later flourishing under Ratan Tata's stewardship. TCS was founded in 1968 as Tata Computer Systems, a division within Tata Sons. Its initial mandate was to provide computer services to other Tata Group subsidiaries. The company's first assignment was providing punched card services to Tata Steel (then TISCO). This humble start laid the foundation for what would become India's largest IT services company.

In 1969 or 1970, TCS began to expand its horizons beyond the Tata Group. It secured its first domestic project, developing an inter-branch reconciliation system for the central bank of India. This project marked TCS's entry into the banking sector – an industry that would later become one of its strongest verticals. TCS's ambitions were not limited to the Indian market alone, a significant milestone was TCS's partnership with Burroughs, one of the first business computer manufacturers in the world. This collaboration led to TCS writing code for Burroughs machines for several US-based clients. The important experience gained from this partnership proved invaluable as it helped TCS secure its first onsite project with the Institutional Group & Information Company (IGIC). In 1974, the company pioneered the global delivery model for IT services with its first offshore client in a revolutionary move that set the stage for India's emergence as a global IT services hub.

Recognizing the importance of research and development in the rapidly evolving IT landscape, TCS established the Tata Research Development and Design Centre (TRDDC) in Pune in 1981. This was India's first software research centre. It has since been at the forefront of software engineering, process engineering, and systems research in the country. One of TRDDC's most noteworthy achievements was the development of MasterCraft, a model-driven development software application that can automatically create and rewrite codes based on user needs.

The Ratan Tata Era of TCS

When Ratan Tata took the helm of the Tata Group in 1991, he was rightly able to predict the immense potential of the IT sector. Under his leadership, TCS underwent a significant transformation from a domestic-focused entity to a global IT services powerhouse.

In 1992, Ratan Tata initiated several strategic partnerships to bolster TCS's capabilities. A notable collaboration was with IBM, which marked Tata's entry into information technology solutions tailored for Indian businesses. This partnership enhanced TCS's ability to develop cutting-edge IT solutions and compete in the global IT market.

The 1990s also presented unique opportunities for TCS in the form of the Y2K bug and the launch of the Euro. TCS capitalized on these challenges by pioneering a factory model for Y2K conversion and developing software tools that automated the conversion process. This approach not only solved critical problems for clients but also showcased TCS's ability to handle large-scale and complex projects. Correctly anticipating the dot-com boom, TCS established its e-business division in 2000 with just ten people. This forward-thinking move guided by Ratan Tata paid off handsomely. By 2004, the e-business division was contributing half a billion dollars to TCS's annual revenue, demonstrating Ratan's acumen in identifying and making the most of emerging trends.

One of the most significant events in TCS's history occurred on 9 August 2004, when the company went public. This initial public offering (IPO) was a landmark event at the time, raising ₹4,713 crore, which resulted in TCS becoming the first billion-dollar IPO in Indian history. The successful listing provided TCS with considerable capital for further expansion while also demonstrating the company's maturity and market confidence. Under Ratan Tata's leadership, TCS achieved several financial milestones. For instance, in 2006, it crossed $4 billion in annual revenue, and by 2012, this figure had more than doubled with TCS surpassing $10 billion in annual revenue.

Ratan Tata's vision for TCS extended beyond organic growth. The company made several strategic acquisitions to expand its global footprint and enhance its service offerings. Notable acquisitions included Financial Network Services (FNS) in Australia (2005), which added core-banking solutions to TCS's portfolio; Citigroup Global Services Limited (2008), which significantly enhanced TCS's banking and financial services domain knowledge; and

Supervalu Services India (2010), which strengthened TCS's retail sector capabilities. These important acquisitions both expanded TCS's geographical presence and deepened its expertise in key emerging industry verticals.

Under Ratan Tata's guidance, TCS continued to give precedence to innovation. In 2006, the company launched its co-innovation network (COIN), which aimed to connect innovation labs, start-up alliances, university research departments and venture capitalists. This initiative fostered a culture of novel ideas and collaboration with TCS being at the forefront of technological advancements in India. TCS also established nineteen innovation labs across three countries in prominent partnerships with prestigious institutions like the IITs in India and Stanford University, MIT and Carnegie Mellon in the US. These collaborations ensured that TCS remained connected to leading-edge research and technologies.

Ratan Tata's leadership successfully metamorphosized TCS from a primarily India-focused company into a global IT services giant. By the time he stepped down as chairman in 2012, TCS had become the crown jewel of the Tata Group that continues to contribute a large proportion of the Group's market capitalisation and global reputation. It is not an exaggeration to say that Ratan Tata had a direct impact on the current form of TCS's reputation. With over 6,01,000 consultants across 55 countries and annual revenues of US $29.1 billion as of 31 March 2024, TCS continues to be a global leader in IT services, consulting and business solutions. The company's success has been crucial in establishing India as a global IT powerhouse.

CHAPTER 5

LEGACY AND VALUES

- Philanthropy and Social Impact
- Commitment to Ethical Leadership
- Mentorship and Influence on Emerging Entrepreneurs

Philanthropy and Social Impact

Ratan Tata's legacy has been defined by his profound commitment to philanthropy and social impact, which has touched millions of lives in India. As the steward of the Tata Trusts, one of India's oldest and largest charitable institutions, Ratan Tata transformed the organization's focus to address a wide range of pressing social issues. His vision of inclusive growth and corporate social responsibility became the cornerstone of the Tata Group's ethos, which set a new standard for ethical business practices worldwide.

Under Ratan's leadership, the trusts expanded their reach to healthcare, education, rural development and innovation, with initiatives that ranged from building state-of-the-art cancer treatment facilities to supporting groundbreaking research in neurosciences. His personal investments in start-ups with social impact and his generous donations to educational institutions worldwide reflect his deep-seated belief that the corporate sector should contribute to societal progress as well.

Tata's philanthropic efforts came to the forefront during times of crisis, most notably during the Covid-19 pandemic, when he pledged substantial resources to support India's fight against the virus. This chapter explores the multifaceted nature of Ratan Tata's philanthrophy and the lasting impact it has had on society, embodying his philosophy that a company's success is intrinsically linked to the welfare of the community it serves.

1. Tata Medical Center

The Tata Medical Center, an advanced cancer care and research facility in Kolkata, was inaugurated by Ratan Tata in 2011. This philanthropic initiative was undertaken by Ratan to address the critical need for advanced cancer treatment in eastern India and neighbouring countries. The hospital is a sprawling property spread over 13 acres in Rajarhat, providing comprehensive cancer care and also offering cancer treatment to underprivileged patients at significantly subsidized rates. With an initial capacity of 150 beds, the centre was expanded to over 400 beds under a phase-II expansion drive. A key feature of the Tata Medical Center is its commitment to accessible healthcare. Half of the beds are available for free or at subsidized rates to poor patients to address the high cost of cancer treatment. This aligns with Ratan Tata's lifelong belief in making quality healthcare affordable to all sections of society.

The centre not only focuses on treatment but also on research and education. In 2014, the Tata Translational Cancer Research Centre (TTCRC) was established on a two-acre plot within

Tata Medical Center, Kolkata, West Bengal, India

the hospital complex to foster a supportive environment for clinicians, scientists and industry to collaborate on cancer research. To support patients and their families coming from outside Kolkata, the hospital features a facility called Premashraya that can accommodate more than 200 patients.

The Tata Medical Center has made significant strides in cancer care since its inception. It receives around six hundred new patients every day and has become a beacon of hope for cancer patients from the eastern region and neighbouring countries like Bangladesh and Bhutan. Under Ratan Tata's guidance, the centre has also focused on building partnerships and raising funds to sustain its mission. To date, several major corporate houses, industrialists and even Bollywood celebrities have made substantial financial contributions to the center's fundraising efforts. The establishment of the Tata Medical Center is exemplary in reflecting Ratan Tata's commitment to addressing critical healthcare needs of underserved regions and populations, especially the provision of high-quality medical care, as well as his sense of responsibility regarding utilizing the Tata Group's resources and expertise to create lasting social impact.

2. Affordable Cancer Treatment Facilities

In 2017, under Ratan Tata's guidance, the Tata Trusts launched an ambitious Cancer Care Programme, introducing the Distributed Cancer Care Model. The objective of this initiative was to create a network of cancer care centers and screening facilities in smaller cities and towns, especially to address the critical need for accessible and affordable cancer treatment across the nation. The programme's vision was to reverse the alarming statistic that around 70 per cent of cancer cases in India are diagnosed at late stages, which often worsens the patients' chances of survival. Ratan Tata's goal was to flip this ratio, aiming for 70 per cent of cases to be diagnosed in the early stages when cancer treatment is more effective and less costly.

A key component of this initiative was the partnership between the Tata Trusts and the Government of Assam. In 2018, they signed an MoU to construct seventeen cancer hospitals across Assam. This network was strategically designed to serve not only Assam but the entire North East, ensuring that patients from bordering states could also access these services.

By 2023, significant progress was made. Seven hospitals in Barpeta, Dibrugarh, Tezpur, Lakhimpur, Jorhat, Kokrajhar and Darrang became functional on 28 April 2022. These facilities have already made a substantial impact; for instance, up to August 2023; 2,78,344 people were screened for common cancers, with 211 confirmed cases. During this period, the hospitals registered 31,005 patients and delivered 18,319 chemotherapy sessions and 62,160 radiation therapy sessions under government schemes, resulting in no financial burden to the patients.

The programme also focused on developing cost-effective treatments. For instance, the Tata Institute in Mumbai announced the development of a breakthrough treatment that could prevent cancer recurrence, available in tablet form for just ₹100. This initiative reflects Tata's belief that financial barriers should never stand in the way of life-saving treatment.

Ratan Tata's approach included community outreach, early detection initiatives and efforts to improve the overall cancer care ecosystem of the country. The Tata Trusts' Distributed Cancer Care Model aimed to bring high-quality cancer care closer to patients' homes in an effort to reduce the need for long-distance travel and the associated costs. By combining the resources of the Tata Trusts with government partnerships and innovative approaches, Ratan Tata was able to set in motion a programme that could revolutionize cancer care in India by making it more accessible, affordable and effective for millions of patients.

3. Tata Education and Development Trust

The Tata Education and Development Trust was established in 2008 by Ratan Tata with the objective of advancing education and fostering global connections. This philanthropic arm of the Tata Group has made substantial contributions to educational institutions both in India and abroad.

One of the trust's most notable initiatives was the establishment of the Tata Scholarship Fund at Cornell University in 2008. With a generous endowment of $28 million, this fund was created to provide financial aid for undergraduate students from India. This is a prime example of Ratan Tata's commitment to enabling talented Indian students to access world-class education regardless of their financial circumstances.

The scholarship programme at Cornell is particularly significant given Ratan Tata's personal connection to the university, where he earned his degree in architecture in 1962. By creating this opportunity for Indian students, Ratan Tata not only gave back to his alma mater but also opened doors for future generations of scholars from India.

The trust's impact goes well beyond the individual scholarships. In 2010, it made a landmark donation of $50 million to Harvard Business School for the construction of Tata Hall, an executive education complex. This underscores Ratan Tata's lifelong belief in the importance of global business education and leadership development.

In India, the trust has been instrumental in supporting various educational initiatives. For example, it has contributed to the development of institutions such as the Indian Institute of Technology Bombay. In 2014, the trust provided a grant of ₹950 million to IIT Bombay to establish the Tata Centre for Technology and Design (TCTD).

The trust's commitment to advancing scientific research is evident in its support for the Centre for Neuroscience at the Indian Institute of Science. In 2014, it provided a grant of ₹750 million to study mechanisms underlying Alzheimer's disease and to develop methods for its early diagnosis and treatment. Under Ratan Tata's guidance, the trust has improved the quality of education at the grassroots level. It has supported several initiatives to enhance teacher training, improve school infrastructure and introduce innovative teaching methodologies in rural and underprivileged areas.

The Tata Education and Development Trust's work exemplifies

Ratan Tata's philosophy of using education as a tool for social transformation. By supporting institutions and individuals across the educational spectrum - ranging from primary schools in rural India to Ivy League universities in the US – the trust has created a lasting impact on education.

4. Tata Centre for Technology and Design

The Tata Centre for Technology and Design (TCTD) was established in 2014 at the IIT Bombay to foster technological advancements that help address societal issues. This initiative was launched with considerable support from the Tata Trusts and had the primary objective of developing and designing technology solutions that meet the unfulfilled requirements of resource-constrained communities.

The centre operates on an end-to-end innovation approach and often acts as a virtual hub that draws faculty members and graduate students from various departments across IIT Bombay. This interdisciplinary approach ensures a holistic perspective in addressing complex societal problems. One of the key features of TCTD is its focus on creating solutions that are technologically advanced, economically viable and socially relevant. The centre's projects span various fields, with the most important being agriculture and food, education, environment, health, housing, water and waste management.

Under Ratan Tata's guidance and within six years of its inception, the centre had around 45 active projects and 30 applications in the invention disclosure process for relevant patents, copyrights and trademarks. The TCTD also places a strong emphasis on nurturing future leaders in technology and social innovation, such as through the support and training it provides to MTech students and PhD scholars, grooming them to become leaders familiar with developmental challenges in the Indian sociopolitical context. By 2020, the number of Tata Fellows had grown to ninety-five, with about twenty fellows graduating that year.

An innovative aspect of the TCTD's approach is the TCTD Yatra, wherein Tata Fellows experience community living and observe how social enterprises scale up using technology, operational efficiencies and trained human resources. This hands-on experience ensures that the solutions developed are grounded in real-world contexts and that the research can be adapted into practical applications. Six start-ups have emerged from TCTD projects, with entrepreneurs often evolving from its research teams. Beyond Mumbai, TCTD also conducts several courses in end-to-end innovation for academic circles and organizes workshops that have benefited over 1,250 faculty members and students from engineering colleges across India. Through the establishment of TCTD, Ratan Tata succeeded in creating a platform that bridges the gap between academic research and real-world challenges, especially those specific to India.

5. Small Animal Hospital in Mumbai

The Small Animal Hospital in Mumbai, inaugurated on 1 July 2023, is a cutting-edge and infrastructurally advanced pet hospital located in Mahalaxmi, Mumbai. This veterinary hospital was Ratan Tata's last major philanthropic project. It was close to his heart and is considered his personal tribute to animal care.

Spanning an impressive 98,000 square feet over five floors, the ₹165-crore facility is the first of its kind in India. It offers 24/7 emergency care and is equipped with advanced technology, including ICUs and HDUs, with the ability to provide life support for critically ill and injured animals, as well as modern diagnostic imaging services like CT scans, MRIs, X-rays and ultrasound.

Legend has it that Ratan once had to fly his dog to the University of Minnesota for a joint replacement surgery but arrived too late for the procedure. This experience stayed with him, and over time, it inspired him to set up top-notch healthcare for pets in India. To this end, the hospital is designed to cater to a wide range of veterinary needs and includes surgery units; specialty treatments in areas like dermatology, dental care and ophthalmology; an in-house pathology lab; and separate waiting areas for dogs and cats.

A key aspect of the hospital's mission that Ratan Tata oversaw personally was to provide healthcare and treatment to stray animals. For this purpose, the hospital has current plans to construct an annexe dedicated to the sterilization and treatment of stray dogs that will run in partnership with the NGO Welfare of Stray Dogs. The hospital operates completely on a not-for-profit model that aligns with Ratan Tata's immense love and reverence for animal lives. Dr Thomas Heathcote, the chief veterinary officer and CEO of the Advanced Veterinary Care Foundation (AVCF), which runs the facility, described the opening of this hospital as 'one of the most exhilarating experiences' of his career.

The impact of the hospital has been felt community-wide, with pet owners often describing it as a godsend for emergency animal healthcare in Mumbai and praising the expertise and kindness of the staff. Indian celebrities, such as Shilpa Shetty, have also publicly appreciated the facility after their pets received treatment there.

A second phase of the hospital's development is already being planned. This will include specialized surgeries, such as orthopaedic and laparoscopic work, complex medical management, physiotherapy and advanced oncology. This would be a direct realization of Ratan Tata's vision for compassionate animal care, ensuring that his love for animals continues to make a tangible difference in the lives of animals and their human companions alike.

6. Covid-19 Relief Fund

In response to the unprecedented global health crisis triggered by the Covid-19 pandemic, Ratan Tata demonstrated exemplary leadership by spearheading a massive relief effort through the Tata Trusts and Tata Group. On 28 March 2020, the Tata Trusts announced a donation of ₹500 crore (approximately $66 million at the time) to fight the coronavirus pandemic. Ratan Tata had personally announced this significant contribution, describing the Covid-19 crisis as 'one of the toughest challenges that the human race will face'. This initial commitment was quickly followed by an additional pledge of ₹1,000 crore from Tata Sons, bringing the total contribution from the Tata Group to ₹1,500 crore.

Here are some of his relief efforts for addressing critical needs arising from the pandemic:

- Personal protective equipment (PPE): The trusts focused on procuring and distributing PPE for medical personnel working tirelessly on the frontlines.

- Testing kits: Efforts were made to increase the availability of testing kits to enhance India's per capita testing capacity.
- Treatment facilities: The trusts worked on creating modular facilities for the provision of Covid-19 care and improving the availability of treatment centres.
- Professional training: Programmes were initiated to enhance the capabilities of healthcare professionals to respond effectively to the crisis.
- Community outreach: A countrywide campaign was launched to build knowledge and increase resilience in communities with the expectation of reaching twelve million people in twenty-one states.

Under this initiative, various Tata companies also contributed by repurposing their facilities and resources to aid in the fight against Covid-19. For example, Tata Motors converted one of its plants to manufacture ventilators while Tata Steel's food services worked to provide meals to migrant workers and daily wage earners.

During this crisis, Ratan Tata's formidable leadership shone through in his focus on effectively utilizing emergency healthcare resources for fighting the pandemic in India. The impact of his initiatives was significant, with the Tata Steel Foundation's 10-point #CombatCovid19 programme impacting more than 10.5 lakh people across India during the first wave of the pandemic. Moreover, in early 2021, when the programme was recalibrated, it reached over 4.5 lakh additional people.

7. Scholarships for Underprivileged Students

Staying true to his commitment to social upliftment through education, Ratan Tata was responsible for establishing numerous scholarship initiatives aimed at providing educational opportunities to talented students from financially disadvantaged backgrounds. One of the most significant initiatives in this regard is the Tata Scholarship at Cornell University. Similarly, the Sir Ratan Tata Post-doctoral Fellowship at the London School of Economics (LSE) is another noteworthy fellowship that provides Indian scholars with the opportunity to engage in research on south Asian issues at LSE for six months.

During Ratan Tata's tenure as chairman, the Tata Group initiated countless scholarships and fellowships within India. The impact of these scholarship programmes is demonstrated by a generation of professionals who have emerged from these programmes and gone on to make significant contributions on the global stage. Ratan Tata also supported initiatives such as Tata STRIVE, which is a skill development programme to provide young Indians with industry-relevant skills. Impacting thousands of marginalized youths, it has provided them with the confidence and skills necessary for finding gainful employment.

8. Rural Development Initiatives

Ratan Tata felt that rural development was very important for the nation's overall upliftment. Under his guidance, the Tata Group started numerous initiatives in rural areas of India, particularly those experiencing endemic poverty.

One of the most significant programmes in this realm is the Transforming Rural India (TRI) initiative by the Tata Trusts. This comprehensive programme works to trigger a large-scale transformation of villages, especially in states like Madhya Pradesh, Jharkhand and Chhattisgarh. It operates through partnerships with leading non-profit organizations, state governments, market players, civil society and private philanthropies to provide a range of services.

In the field of health and nutrition, TRI has implemented interventions across 342 villages in Madhya Pradesh, covering a thousand habitations. It has also provided training to hundreds of volunteers in community-led protocols, initiating discussions with over 2,000 women's groups in their respective villages. Education has been another key focus area of the TRI initiative, with many educational interventions spanning primary schools in 566 villages in Madhya Pradesh. An MoU was signed with the Department of Education, Government of Madhya Pradesh, to drive engagement with teachers and schools, which resulted in the provision of support to 198 schools and 731 community volunteers working with village organizations.

In the agricultural sector, the TRI initiative Kushal Kisan Abhiyaan has worked to promote the adoption of commercial agriculture techniques using rural media channels. This programme was started in three administrative blocks of Jharkhand, which covers thousands of farmers. As a result, around 630 farmers were able to increase their incomes by over ₹1,00,000, and 98 agri-entrepreneurs were engaged as Value Chain Actors. Additionally, the initiative fosters youth empowerment through the Sarathi platform, which supports young aspirants from villages in Madhya Pradesh, Jharkhand and Chhattisgarh by helping them make informed career choices and connecting them to a pool of screened trainers. A key aspect of the TRI initiative is preparing conservation and development strategies for particularly vulnerable tribal groups through an annual funding of ₹1 billion and in collaboration with the Tribal Welfare Department of the Government of Madhya Pradesh.

In line with Ratan Tata's vision, the TRI plans to reach 1,00,000 villages in 1,000 blocks and potentially transform two hundred million lives. Moreover, the programme aims to intensify activities to enhance the quality of life of 25 per cent of outreach households, expand market solutions, increase government engagement in countering societal problems and diversify livelihood opportunities.

9. Sanitation and Clean Water Projects and the Tata Water Mission

During his lifetime, Ratan Tata ensured that the Tata Group worked to address India's critical water and sanitation challenges, particularly through the Tata Water Mission (TWM). This comprehensive initiative focuses on three key components – water, sanitation and hygiene (WaSH) – along with working towards rainwater conservation, sustainability of water sources and increasing access to clean water.

The TWM's ambitious scale encompasses operations in several Indian states, including Rajasthan, Gujarat, Maharashtra, Karnataka, Andhra Pradesh, Jharkhand, Assam, Nagaland, Mizoram, Uttar Pradesh, Uttarakhand, Himachal Pradesh, Punjab and in the union territory of Ladakh. Its strategy includes using technological advancements to address water quality issues. To this end, the trusts have identified and piloted technologies to remove arsenic and fluoride from water in Assam and Rajasthan. Through collaboration with the central and state governments, the trusts have made significant attempts to make rural communities self-sustainable for their basic water, sanitation and hygiene needs. The Zila Swachh Bharat Programme, a fellowship programme that supports the government's Swachh Bharat Mission (Gramin), was started by the Tata Trusts to train and employ over five hundred professionals to assist district collectorates in their work to mitigate sanitation challenges.

Various Tata Group companies have also been involved in TWM. For example, Tata Chemicals supported over 50,000 households by selling Tata Swachh water purifiers through rural social entrepreneurs in Nagaland, Mizoram, Arunachal Pradesh and Assam. Similarly, Tata AIG funded the use of mechanical equipment for safer cleaning of sewers, and Tata Capital provided funding to the Mission Garima project of Plan India to ensure non-hazardous work environments for sanitation workers. Other collaborative efforts under TMW include Tata AIA's menstrual hygiene programme in Maharashtra and Rajasthan, Titan Company's support for the TWM in Uttarakhand and Tata Consumer Products, funding of TMW in Assam and Himachal Pradesh.

10. Maternal and Child Healthcare Programmes

Ratan Tata's desire to improve the public healthcare system in India has been prominently reflected in the Tata Trusts' focus on Reproductive, Maternal, Neonatal, Child and Adolescent Healthcare (RMNCHA+). To this end, the Tata Trusts' RMNCHA+ programme operates in eight districts across Madhya Pradesh and Rajasthan and covers over eighty healthcare facilities.

Under this programme, the trusts provide training to Accredited Social Health Activists (ASHAs) and Auxiliary Nurse Midwives (ANMs) regarding the identification and treatment of high-risk pregnancies, which can help reduce maternal mortality. Additionally, it has been working on identifying and resolving infrastructural gaps in maternal, newborn and child health facilities in impoverished areas. The programme also aims to use technology to implement helpful interventions at a large scale in a cost-effective manner and monitor the performance of the programme. Under this project, the provision of timely treatment during pregnancy has been able to effectively prevent maternal deaths through potential causes, such as post-partum haemorrhage, sepsis and hypertensive disorders. For neonatal care, the programme works to mitigate issues like premature births, infections (pneumonia and septicaemia) and asphyxia.

Here are two other major initiatives in this space undertaken by the Tata Trusts:

I. ĀSMĀN (Alliance for Saving Mothers and Newborns): This is a collaboration between the Tata Trusts, the Bill and Melinda Gates Foundation, US Agency for International Development (USAID), Merck Sharp & Dohme (MSD) and Reliance Foundation. This alliance mentors nurses through modern technology including audio-visual tutorials and gamification modules, provides a digital checklist for facilities to identify gaps in infrastructure and nurse training and call centres with doctors and nurses available 24x7.

II. As a lead development partner of the Government of Madhya Pradesh, the trust offers training to auxiliary nurse midwives. At more than 700 delivery points in the state, this project aims to train over four thousand medical professionals on how to deal with high-risk pregnancies and at-risk live births. The trust has built an application called Systematic Enabler for Health Action and Transformation (SEHAT) for this purpose.

11. Tata Innovation Centre at Cornell Tech

The Tata Innovation Centre at Cornell Tech, inaugurated in 2017, came to fruition due to Ratan Tata's desire to propagate innovation in both academia and industry. This state-of-the-art facility was formerly known as the Bridge and is designed to bring together academic researchers and industry professionals under one roof and promote the exchange of ideas. The centre was renamed in honour of Tata Consultancy Services after it made a significant donation of $50 million for technology research at Cornell Tech and the expansion of K-12 digital literacy programmes in New York City.

The centre serves multiple purposes: It is a hub for New York's tech sector, as well as a focal point for technological advancements by diverse stakeholders; it provides crucial support for innovation activities at Cornell Tech and for enhancing the institution's capacity for research and development; it works to boost economic competitiveness by promoting collaboration between academia and industry; it houses research teams working on emerging areas such as human–machine interaction and cybersecurity; it accommodates several companies working alongside Cornell academic teams; and TCS and Cornell Tech have partnered to promote computational expertise and digital fluency in K-12 schools across New York City.

Dan Huttenlocher, who was dean of Cornell Tech, noted that the institute's partnership with TCS has significantly enhanced its ability to make measurable difference in areas ranging from commercialization of research to engaging with public school students across New York City.

12. Tata Hall at Harvard Business School

Tata Hall at Harvard Business School (HBS) is a modern facility that was made possible through a generous $50 million donation from Tata companies, the Sir Dorabji Tata Trust and the Tata Education and Development Trust. The seven-story, glass-and-limestone structure spans 1,63,000 square feet and is designed to enhance HBS's executive education programme. It features 179 bedrooms for executive education participants, two classrooms that can seat ninety-nine students each and multiple gathering spaces and conference rooms.

Ratan Tata, a 1975 graduate of HBS's advanced management programme, played a significant role in the building's conception. As an architect himself, Tata presented two design challenges to the firm behind Tata Hall – making the building warm and welcoming to visitors and ensuring it as open and transparent as possible. The resulting design features extensive use of glass, allowing the building to 'touch the ground lightly', according to Tata's vision for it. The hall was completed in late 2013 and it incorporates several environment-friendly features, such as a low-flow plumbing system, a solar array for air conditioning power and LEED Platinum certification.

During the dedication ceremony, Ratan Tata reflected on his own experience at HBS, describing his initial thirteen weeks in the advanced management programme as transformative. He candidly shared that he initially felt 'confused' and 'humiliated' by the impressive calibre of his fellow students, but later recognized this period as 'the most important 13 weeks' of his life.

Commenting on the significance of Tata's contribution, HBS dean Nitin Nohria referred to the hall as 'by far the most significant gift made by an international alum' to the school. This is because the hall's construction has enabled HBS to accommodate more than 9,000 students annually in a collaborative learning environment.

13. Support for Anti-Sikh Pogrom Victims

In the aftermath of the 1984 anti-Sikh pogrom in India, Ratan Tata and the Tata Group demonstrated exceptional compassion and support for the affected Sikh community. This humanitarian gesture left a lasting impact on the lives of many Sikh families and earned the group their enduring loyalty and respect.

The 1984 anti-Sikh violence resulted in the loss of thousands of lives and livelihoods, particularly affecting Sikh truck drivers whose vehicles were destroyed in the riots. In response to this crisis, Tata Motors (then known as TELCO) made the notable decision to gift new trucks to Sikh drivers who had lost their vehicles. This act of kindness was never publicized and only came to light in recent years. According to Abhiraj Singh Bhal, co-founder and CEO of Urban Company, a Sikh driver recounted to him how Tata Motors provided him with a new truck with no questions asked after his previous vehicle was set ablaze. Decades later, many Sikh drivers remain loyal customers of Tata trucks, demonstrating the long-lasting goodwill generated by Ratan Tata's compassionate action. This lesser-known chapter in Ratan Tata's philanthropic journey highlights his desire to take swift and practical actions for pressing social problems, even in politically sensitive situations.

14. Healthcare Initiatives of the Tata Trusts

The Tata Trusts have made significant contributions to healthcare in India under Ratan Tata's leadership. One of the most notable healthcare initiatives is the Cancer Care Programme, which includes the Tata Memorial Hospital in Mumbai, Tata Medical Center in Kolkata and the New Tata Memorial Centre hospitals in Varanasi and the North East. In addition to these, the Distributed Cancer Care Model was launched in 2017 to create a network of cancer care centres and screening facilities in smaller cities and towns.

The Tata Trusts have also supported various programmes on improving maternal and child health, especially in rural areas. Ratan Tata was a vocal advocate for awareness and support of mental health and fostered several collaborations with organizations like the National Institute of Mental Health and Neurosciences (NIMHANS) to implement mental health programmes for depression, anxiety and substance abuse.

In March 2018, the trusts initiated a programme in Mathura, Uttar Pradesh, to provide primary healthcare to rural populations through eleven telemedicine units (TMUs) and two mobile medical units (MMUs). This initiative focuses on preventing non-communicable diseases such as cardiovascular diseases, diabetes and hypertension.

We have already learnt about Tata's initiatives to combat the Covid-19 menace. By focusing on both immediate healthcare needs and long-term research and development, the Tata Trusts have made a lasting impact on the Indian healthcare system in terms of accessibility, affordability and quality of medical care.

Commitment to Ethical Leadership

Ratan Tata's tenure as the chairman of the Tata Group and his continued influence as chairman emeritus after retirement has been characterized by his unwavering commitment to propagating ethical leadership and sustainability. His vision to this end has helped shape the Tata Group into a global powerhouse in relation to its corporate responsibility efforts and sustainable practices.

When Ratan Tata succeeded J.R.D. Tata as chairman, he took the Group's legacy of ethical practices further by highlighting the need for sustainability alongside profitability. In 1992, as he began to consolidate his leadership, he articulated a vision for the Tata Group that placed ethical conduct and environmental responsibility at its core. This commitment was formalized in 2000 with the establishment of the Tata Group Environment Network, which was designed to strengthen conservation efforts across all Tata companies, marking a significant step towards integrating environmental considerations into the Group's business strategies. The network facilitated knowledge sharing and best practices among Tata companies and promoted a culture of environmental stewardship.

In 2002, the Tata Group published its first 'Report on Tata Environment', a groundbreaking document that featured case studies on biodiversity and environmental issues from fifteen Group companies. This report covered the Group's ongoing environmental initiatives, as well as provided new standards for corporate transparency in environmental matters. Building on this momentum, in 2004, Ratan Tata directed sixteen Tata companies to participate in the Global Reporting Initiative (GRI) – a worldwide autonomous standards-setting body with the primary role of assisting corporations, governmental entities and organizations in comprehending and effectively conveying their influence on crucial global issues, including environmental changes, fundamental human rights and unethical practices in governance. By aligning with GRI guidelines, Tata companies began to systematically measure, disclose and be accountable for their environmental, social and governance impact.

The launch of the Tata Nano project in 2007 was a prime example of Ratan Tata's wish to make mobility affordable for millions of Indians through inclusivity. Next year, the 26/11 Mumbai terror attacks devastated the entire nation, and Ratan Tata's leadership during the attack was evident through his tireless efforts to save employees and guests alike. As the terrorists targeted the iconic Taj Hotel owned by the Tata Group, Ratan Tata personally oversaw the relief efforts being conducted, exhibiting immense empathy and courage. His hands-on approach during this crisis was to prioritize the safety of guests and employees over business concerns, which earned him even more widespread respect.

In 2009, under Ratan Tata's guidance, the Group introduced the Tata Climate Change Policy. This policy set industry benchmarks for carbon footprint reduction and climate change advocacy, effectively positioning the Tata Group as a leader in corporate climate action. The policy outlines specific targets for reducing greenhouse gas emissions and increasing the use of renewable energy across Tata companies. Recognizing the intrinsic link between climate change and biodiversity, Ratan

Tata established a knowledge partnership between the Group and the Bombay Natural History Society. This collaboration contributes to developing multi-year perspectives on biodiversity conservation through the integration of scientific research and environmental protection strategies.

In 2014, Ratan Tata's vision for sustainable business practices led to the formation of the Tata Sustainability Group – a dedicated entity tasked with encapsulating sustainability principles into the business strategies of all Tata companies, with environmental and social considerations being integral to decision-making processes. The next year marked two significant milestones to this end. First, Ratan Tata signed an open letter on climate change as part of the CEO Climate Leaders Coalition, joining global business leaders in calling for worldwide urgent action on climate change. Second, the Group introduced the Tata Sustainability Policy, a comprehensive document outlining the Group's aspiration to be a global sustainability leader. This document provided a framework for Tata companies to integrate sustainability into their operations, especially through climate change mitigation, resource conservation and community development.

In 2017, Ratan Tata was responsible for the Tata Group publishing its first Sustainable Development Goals (SDGs) report, becoming the first Indian corporate to do so. This report detailed how Tata companies have been contributing to the United Nations' global sustainability goals through its business practices and international development programmes.

Ratan Tata's decades-long commitment to ethical leadership received global recognition in 2020 when he was conferred the title of 'Global Visionary of Sustainable Business and

Peace'. Apart from the above initiatives taken by Ratan Tata to help people afflicted by Covid-19, the Tata Trusts pledged an additional ₹75 crore to support online education and digital learning tools for underprivileged children in a bid to address the educational challenges brought on by the pandemic.

> **IN 2022, THE TATA GROUP RANKED NO. 1 IN ASIA PACIFIC IN THE GLOBESCAN SUSTAINABILITY LEADERS SURVEY, IN NO SMALL PART THANKS TO RATAN TATA'S VISION.**

As of 2024, Ratan Tata's legacy continues to be celebrated for his prioritization of ethical leadership, philanthropy and sustainability, which can rightly be considered the defining features of his career. From formalizing environmental reporting to championing climate change policies, from innovating for social inclusivity to responding compassionately during crises, Ratan Tata has consistently and successfully demonstrated that entrepreneurial success and ethical conduct are not mutually exclusive. His leadership is also a shining example of the fact that corporations can be powerful agents of positive change, which has set new standards for business leaders to be ethical in their practices.

Mentorship and Influence on Emerging Entrepreneurs

Ratan Tata's influence extends far beyond his role as the chairman of Tata Sons; his legacy continues through the roles he played as a mentor, adviser and inspiration to several emerging entrepreneurs and leaders. His mentorship style was characterized by a unique blend of wisdom, humility and a genuine interest in nurturing talent and providing personal guidance.

Abhiraj Singh Bhal, co-founder of Urban Company, recalls his first meeting with Ratan Tata during which the latter provided him with advice regarding Bhal's new start-up, which was then called Urban Clap. Bhal recalled, 'He said, "Abhiraj, Varun and Raghav, you are building something that India needs. Just make sure that you keep the quality really, really high, and the rest will follow ... if you would give me the opportunity, I would love to partner with you as a small shareholder."' Today, Urban Company is a major success story that benefited hugely from Tata's guidance and encouragement.

In the decade following his retirement as chairman of Tata Group, Ratan Tata invested in over forty start-ups across various sectors. His focus was not just on financial returns; he wanted to continue encouraging innovation and novel ideas that could benefit society. Ratan Tata often viewed these investments as opportunities to learn and gain insights into emerging trends.

One of his notable investments was in Ola, which is now India's leading ride-hailing service. In July 2015, he made a personal investment of ₹95 lakhs in the company, and later, his investment firm, RNT Capital Advisers, invested an additional ₹400 crore. His support also extended to Ola Electric, the company's electric vehicle venture. Bhavish Aggarwal, Ola's co-founder and CEO, has acknowledged Tata's monumental role as an inspiration and mentor in Ola's journey.

Paytm is another significant investment that exhibits Tata's foresight in the fintech sector. He invested in One97

Communications, Paytm's parent company, in March 2015. In addition to the capital, he also took on an advisory role, which was instrumental in transforming Paytm from a mobile recharge platform to a fintech giant. Vijay Shekhar Sharma, Paytm's CEO, described Tata as 'the most humble businessman in India' and highlighted the impact of his mentorship on his successful career.

Lenskart, an online eyewear retailer, received Tata's backing in April 2016. Despite the relatively small investment of around ₹10 lakh, Tata's involvement in guiding and mentoring the company was crucial in its current success.

The impact of Tata's mentorship is best illustrated through the experiences of entrepreneurs who have benefited from his guidance. Anuradha Acharya, founder & CEO of Mapmygenome, shares her experience of meeting Ratan Tata in a poignant social media post after his death:

> It was in 2016, when I was in his office for an investment into Mapmygenome – Know Yourself. I met with his team and he had just landed from the US and was in meetings. I wanted to meet him. They said I would have to wait 3 hours if I wanted to meet to which I happily agreed. It was totally worth it. He actually read details and told me what an important role we are playing for the country. I was on cloud nine but asked if he would like to be a part of our journey to which he smiled and said, let's see.

Neha Singh, co-founder of Tracxn, offers another perspective on Ratan Tata's mentorship style by recalling that her first meeting with him lasted over an hour and she received a call for an investment shortly after. She has also said that the meeting was memorable and that Tata was curious and open to asking questions about her business.

Ratan Tata's approach to supporting start-ups goes beyond mere financial investment, with his involvement often bringing credibility and opening doors for young entrepreneurs. For example, Kaushal Dugar, founder of Teabox, stated that 'literally everyone started taking us seriously in India' and that they were able to receive the much-needed boost to grow due to Ratan Tata coming onboard their business.

This statement highlights the intangible benefits of Tata's involvement in start-ups. One of the key aspects of Tata's mentorship was his emphasis on ethical and social responsibility. He has consistently advocated for businesses to look beyond profit and consider their impact on society. He once famously said, 'I admire people who are very successful. But if that success has been achieved through too much ruthlessness, then I may admire that person less.' His influence on India's start-up ecosystem has also been profound, with his early investments and mentorship often contributing majorly in shaping some of India's most successful start-ups.

Bhavish Aggarwal, co-founder and CEO of Ola, stated, 'Mr Tata was like no other business leader I have ever met. He took personal interest in my journey.' During Aggarwal's mentorship by Ratan Tata, the latter graciously spent a full day in Bengaluru with Aggarwal's team in 2016 and also addressed the company. Expressing his immense gratitude for personally benefitting from Ratan Tata's wisdom, he said, 'I feel so incredibly blessed to have seen such an amazing man from up close, and gotten a chance to see the ideal to strive for.'

Through his mentorship, he enabled many entrepreneurs to realize their potential. His legacy extends far beyond the companies he led or invested in, continuing to live on in the values, practices and aspirations of countless entrepreneurs who were inspired by his example. As India continues to evolve economically, the principles of ethics, social responsibility and innovation that Ratan Tata championed continue to play a crucial role in shaping its future.

Ratan Tata Quotes

Don't wait for opportunities to come to you, create your own opportunities.

Never forget that you are a child of God and you have a right to be here.

Your competition is not other people but the time you kill, the ill will you create, the knowledge you neglect to learn, the connections you fail to build, the health you sacrifice along the path, your inability to generate ideas, the people around you who don't support and love your efforts, and whatever god you curse for your bad luck.

CHAPTER 6

PERSONAL LIFE AND CHARACTER

- Ratan Tata's Personal Traits and Interests
- The Bachelor's Journey: Relationships and Solitude

Personal Traits and Interests

Ratan Tata, the iconic Indian industrialist and philanthropist, was known not just for his business acumen but also for his unique personal qualities and diverse interests.

Humility and Approachability

Many people who worked closely with Ratan Tata have remarked upon his humility and approachability – qualities that set him apart as a leader in the often-ostentatious world of big businesses. Despite his stature as one of India's most influential industrialists, Ratan Tata maintained a down-to-earth demeanour that endeared him to people across all levels of society.

His approachability was particularly evident in his interactions with employees of the Tata Group. He was known to engage with employees and personally encourage a sense of belonging and empowerment within the Tata Group. This approach helped enhance employee morale while also creating a work environment characterized by open communication and collaboration, thereby driving productivity within the organization.

Ratan Tata's humility was not merely a public persona, rather a deeply ingrained aspect of his character. This was exemplified in a notable incident during an induction event for new joiners at the TAS (Tata Administrative Services) leadership programme in 2012. Ratan Tata surprised everyone by kneeling in the front row of people for a group photograph, remarking with humour, 'Please be quick. I can't kneel down for that long.' This left a lasting impression on those present at the event and reinforced his image as a leader who valued and respected everyone.

His modest approach extended beyond formal business settings. Chef and entrepreneur Sanjeev Kapoor recalled an encounter at a US club where Ratan Tata was sitting with his dog without expecting special treatment. This anecdote demonstrates how he was grounded and accessible even in informal settings.

Ratan's humility was also evident in his response to public interactions. In a particularly touching instance, after reaching one million followers on Instagram, he posted a heartfelt thank-you note. In a reply to the post, a follower referred to him as 'Chhotu' (meaning 'small' in Hindi), which drew the ire of people who found it disrespectful. However, Ratan Tata defended the follower and expressed his appreciation for her heartfelt note and also asked other commenters to treat her with respect, revealing his ability to rise above petty criticisms.

The impact of Tata's humble leadership style extended far

beyond the confines of his organization. It set a new standard for leadership in India and globally. He drew the admiration of tech entrepreneur Elon Musk, who referred to Ratan Tata as a true 'gentleman and scholar' during an interview with Charlie Rose.

Ratan Tata's approach to leadership challenged the conventional notion that success in business requires an aggressive or domineering personality. Instead, he demonstrated that humility and approachability are more effective for building trust in both consumers and employees, fostering loyalty and driving sustainable success. The way he led his organization helped create a culture in which his employees felt valued and empowered, making them more productive and innovative.

Integrity and Ethical Standards

Ratan Tata's unwavering commitment to integrity and ethical standards formed the bedrock of his personal and professional life, which raised the standard of corporate governance in India. This steadfast adherence to moral principles was known to inform his decision-making process, which helped cement the Tata Group's reputation as a highly trusted and respected conglomerate.

At the heart of Ratan's ethical framework was his belief in doing the right thing, regardless of the consequences. He often emphasized the importance of ethical decision-making, even when faced with difficult choices. In his own words, 'There will be thousands of occasions when you have to make difficult decisions. You need to, at all times, ask yourself if you are doing the right thing and take the decision that's the right thing, however difficult or unpopular that may be.' This philosophy

In late 2010, the Indian corporate world witnessed the 'Radia Tapes' controversy centring around Niira Radia, a powerful corporate lobbyist whose clients included the Tata Group. The scandal erupted when leaked telephone conversations involving Radia and various high-profile figures, including Ratan Tata, were made public. The tapes were recorded by the Indian Income Tax Department over six months in 2009 and contained over 5,800 conversations with various public figures. Ratan Tata became entangled in the controversy due to Radia's role as the public relations manager for the Tata Group. The leaked conversations revealed Radia discussing various business matters involving Tata and other influential industry figures. Most of Tata and Radia's discussions focused on issues in the telecom sector, particularly concerning A. Raja, telecom minister at that time. The more benign conversations between them covered topics ranging from business and political matters to personal exchanges, such as Tata's dislike for 'black-tie affairs' and light-hearted banter about a Roberto Cavalli gown owned by Radia. In a 2016 *HuffPost* article, Manu Joseph, who previously served as the editor of Open magazine, offered his perspective on the situation. Joseph suggested that while some viewed Tata's reputation to have been damaged by the leaked tapes, this was likely an overstatement, adding that Ratan Tata continued to maintain a respectable public image. Joseph observed that the conversations portrayed Ratan Tata as a wealthy individual attempting to influence policy through a capable but controversial intermediary. However, Joseph also pointed out that Ratan Tata's conduct in these discussions exhibited a certain refined caution, almost as if he were aware of being recorded, though this was likely not the case. For Ratan Tata, who himself was not accused of wrongdoing, the content and tone of the conversations raised questions about corporate ethics and the boundaries of business–government relations. Taking an unusual legal step, Ratan Tata approached the Supreme Court with a petition requesting a thorough inquiry into how the tapes were recorded and leaked to the public. He contended that making these confidential discussions public infringed upon his constitutional right to privacy, as protected under Article 21 of India's Constitution. Ratan Tata also publicly defended his relationship with Radia. In an open letter, he explained that the Tata Group had engaged Radia's firm to counter negative media campaigns orchestrated by rival corporate interests. The Radia Tapes controversy served as a test in crisis management for Ratan Tata as the leak required him to protect corporate interests while maintaining public trust.

guided him in dealing with countless challenging situations throughout his career and earned him respect and admiration from peers and subordinates alike.

Ratan Tata's commitment to ethics was deeply ingrained in his actions and the policies he implemented within the Tata Group. One notable example of this was the Group's response during the 2008 financial crisis. While many companies were struggling to stay afloat, the Tata Group, under Ratan Tata's chairmanship, took several steps to repay their government debts ahead of schedule. This action underscored his commitment to transparency and fairness, particularly during a time of global economic turmoil

The ethical standards set by Ratan Tata permeated every level of the organization. He instituted a comprehensive code of conduct that all Tata employees were expected to adhere to, regardless of their position within the company. This code covered a wide range of ethical considerations ranging from fair business practices to environmental responsibility and social welfare.

Ratan Tata's integrity was also evident in his approach to corporate social responsibility (CSR). Long before CSR became a buzzword in the corporate world, Ratan had already integrated it into the core of his business philosophy. Jamsetji Tata had once stated, 'We do not claim to be more unselfish, more generous or more philanthropic than other people. But we think we started on sound and straightforward business principles, considering the interests of the shareholders our own and the health and welfare of the employees, the sure foundation of our success.' This sentiment was deeply embodied by Ratan Tata during his leadership of numerous philanthropic initiatives, including healthcare and educational programmes, that aimed to improve the lives of communities in which Tata companies operated,

One of the most striking and frequently discussed examples of Ratan Tata's ethical leadership came during the 2008 terrorist attacks in Mumbai. When the Taj Mahal Palace Hotel was captured by a group of terrorists, his immediate concern was for the safety of the guests and staff. In the aftermath, he personally visited the families of all the employees who had been affected by the attack, offered his support and decided to compensate the families of deceased Taj employees through lifelong payment of the employees' salaries. This demonstrated his compassion that extended far beyond legal obligations.

Ratan Tata's commitment to integrity also manifested in his stance against corruption. In a country where corporate bribery and fostering political affiliations through it is often seen as a necessary evil, Ratan Tata took a firm stand against such practices. He once famously stated, 'I will certainly not join politics. I would like to be remembered as a clean businessman who has not partaken in any twists and turns beneath the surface, and one who has been reasonably successful,' adding, 'Power and wealth are not two of my main stakes.' This principled stance sometimes came at a cost as the Group occasionally lost out on business opportunities. However, it also earned the Tata Group a reputation for trustworthiness, which has proven to be invaluable in the long run.

Passion for Innovation

Throughout his career, Ratan Tata demonstrated an unwavering commitment to innovation and a willingness to embrace calculated risks. At the core of his forward-thinking mindset was his belief in the power of creative thinking to drive progress. This encouraged a culture throughout Tata companies wherein bold ideas could flourish and setbacks were perceived as stepping stones to success.

Under Ratan Tata's guidance, the Tata Group nurtured creativity and out-of-the-box thinking. He implemented a three-pronged strategy to enhance innovation across the conglomerate – improving communication and recognition of innovative ideas, facilitating learning from other companies and supporting collaborative research with academia. Perhaps the most iconic example of Tata's innovative drive was the development of the Tata Nano. The inspiration came from a personal observation that he recalled in an Instagram post:

What really motivated me, and sparked a desire to produce such a vehicle, was constantly seeing Indian families on scooters, maybe the child sandwiched between the mother and father, riding to wherever they were going, often on slippery roads.

Although the Nano faced challenges in marketing and perception and was ultimately discontinued, it was a prime example of Tata's desire to create products that improve the lives of common people.

Ratan Tata's innovative approach also shone through in his strategic acquisitions of iconic international brands like Tetley, Jaguar Land Rover and Corus Steel. Moreover, Ratan Tata championed the development of affordable products tailored to emerging markets. To institutionalize innovation, he established various platforms for collaboration both within the Tata ecosystem and with external organizations. The

Group-wide Innovation Forum of the Tata Group organizes events, workshops and interactions between Tata managers, experts and academicians. During his lifetime, Ratan Tata also made substantial investments in research facilities and formed partnerships with academic institutions.

Love for Animals

Ratan Tata was widely known for his immense love for animals, particularly dogs of all kinds, which might just be his most relatable trait for countless Indians. This affection for animals, especially strays, has been a consistent theme throughout his life, which manifested in both his personal actions and philanthropic endeavours.

Ratan Tata used Instagram as a platform to advocate for animal welfare. His posts often featured heartwarming images of dogs, accompanied by messages urging kindness and care for strays. In one such post, he shared a picture of a stray dog seeking shelter from the rain, captioning it with a plea for compassion:

> Now that the monsoons are here, a lot of stray cats and dogs take shelter under our cars. It is important to check under our car before we turn it on and accelerate to avoid injuries to stray animals taking shelter. They can be seriously injured, handicapped and even killed if we are unaware of their presence under our vehicles. It would be heartwarming if we could all offer them temporary shelter when it is pouring this season.

In a landmark initiative, Ratan Tata established the Small Animal Hospital in Mumbai, an advanced facility dedicated to providing high-quality medical care for pets and strays alike. Speaking about this project, Tata stated, 'Pets are our family, and their lives matter to every pet parent. When I looked around and saw the lack of infrastructure for pets in India, it made me wonder why, in such a large country with a significant pet population, we cannot have a facility that can save lives and make pets' lives better.'

Ratan Tata's love for animals was further illustrated in 2018 when he made the decision to cancel a trip to Buckingham Palace, where he was to receive a lifetime award from Prince Charles. He explained to his friend Suhel Seth that one of his dogs had fallen terribly ill, and he did not want to abandon it by leaving for the trip. This incident was widely reported in the media and earned Tata admiration from animal lovers far and wide.

Ratan Tata was known to be actively involved in his dogs' caretaking. He was often seen taking walks with his pets in the Tata Group's office premises in Mumbai, which endeared him to both employees and visitors. Furthermore, with Ratan's influence many Tata companies implemented pet-friendly policies that allowed their employees to bring their pets to work.

Ratan Tata, the Aviation Enthusiast

Ratan Tata loved aviation to the point that it can be considered a defining aspect of his personality. His enthusiasm for flying transcended the boundaries of a casual interest, and his lifelong passion made him achieve remarkable feats in aviation. At the heart of Tata's aviation pursuits was his skill as a pilot, and he held licences to fly both jets and helicopters.

In February 2007, at the age of 69, Ratan Tata etched his name in aviation history by becoming the first Indian civilian to pilot an F-16 Falcon fighter jet. This extraordinary event took place at the Aero India Show in Bengaluru, where he was invited by US defence contractor Lockheed Martin to co-pilot the renowned combat aircraft. The half-hour flight saw Tata taking control of the F-16, soaring through clear skies and reaching altitudes as low as 500 feet. Describing the experience, Tata expressed his amazement saying, 'You end up feeling very timid. We did a few things when the commander took over ... It's just unbelievable.'

Remarkably, the very next day, he took to the skies once more, this time co-piloting Boeing's F-18 Super Hornet – a larger and more powerful aircraft crucial to US Navy operations. This back-to-back experience with two of the world's most advanced fighter jets was a dream come true for Ratan Tata.

Ratan was known to regularly pilot small aircraft and even the company jet. His love for aviation was so intense that he once stated, 'The day I am not able to fly will be a sad day for me.' Tata's aviation expertise even once helped save lives. In 2009, the engine of his single-engine Tri-Pacer failed mid-flight. Demonstrating immense skill and composure, Tata successfully executed an emergency landing, ensuring both his own safety and that of his fellow passengers .

Ratan Tata's experiences and insights as a pilot also informed strategic decisions related to investments in the aviation sector. Under his guidance, the Tata Group formed joint ventures with Air Asia and Singapore Airlines, resulting in the successful launch of Air Asia India and Vistara. Perhaps the crowning achievement of his aviation-related pursuits was the acquisition of Air India in 2022 – a move that brought the airline, originally founded by J.R.D. Tata in 1932 and nationalized in 1953, back into the Tata Group's ownership. For Ratan Tata, this acquisition was the fulfilment of a long-held dream to restore the airline to its former glory under Tata stewardship.

The Bachelor's Journey: Relationships and Solitude

Ratan Tata's personal life, often overshadowed by his several business achievements, reveals a poignant narrative of love, duty and self-sacrifice. Glimpses into his private relationships are few and far between but offer meaningful insights into the man behind the business magnate.

Early Romance and Difficult Choices

Ratan Tata's first significant romantic encounter occurred during his time in Los Angeles, where he worked at an architectural firm after completing his studies at Cornell University. It was here that he met Caroline Jones, daughter of the renowned architect Frederick Earl Emmons. Their relationship blossomed quickly, with Caroline considering Tata her 'first true love'. The couple shared common interests and seemed poised for a future together, with Ratan even contemplating marriage and settling in the United States. However, fate intervened in 1962 when he received news of his grandmother's illness back in India, which forced him to make a difficult choice between his burgeoning romance and family duty. In a candid interview, Tata revealed, 'Well, you know, one was probably the most serious was when I was working in the United States and the only reason we didn't get married was that I came back to India and she was to follow me... and that was the year of the, if you like, the Sino–Indian conflict.' The 1962 Indo–China war created a tense geopolitical situation that made it difficult for Caroline's parents to feel comfortable with her relocating to India.

Ratan Tata's experience with Caroline was not an isolated incident. In a revealing interview with CNN International's Talk Asia, he admitted, 'I came seriously close to getting married four times and each time I backed off in fear or for one reason or another.' Despite his immense success in the business world, Ratan Tata was not immune to the pangs of loneliness that his bachelor life sometimes brought. In a heartfelt conversation with Simi Garewal, he confessed, 'There are many times that I feel lonely about not having a wife or a family, and sometimes I long for it.' This admission was a moment of vulnerability for the industrialist, highlighting the personal sacrifices he made in pursuit of his professional goals and familial duty. Ratan further elaborated on the duality of his solitary life, saying, 'Sometimes I enjoy the freedom of not having to worry about the feelings of someone else or the concerns of someone else. Other times, it does get a little lonely.'

The Return to India and Missed Opportunities

Ratan Tata's return to India in 1962 deeply impacted not only his personal life but also his professional trajectory. Prompted by his grandmother's illness, Ratan made the difficult decision to leave behind a promising relationship and a budding career in the United States – a choice that thrust him into a position of significant responsibility within the Tata Group.

As Ratan Tata immersed himself in the family business, his personal life inevitably took a back seat. The demands of his new role left little room for nurturing romantic relationships. Although according to him, he came close to marriage several more times over the years, each relationship ended with Ratan stepping back.

Reflecting on these moments later in life, Ratan Tata shared that when years later he looked backed at the lives of people he was involved with, he did not believe that he had done 'a bad thing' by ending relationships. The complexities that he alluded to regarding his personal life likely refer to the challenges of balancing a demanding career with marital life.

As Ratan Tata's role within the Tata Group grew, so did the weight of his responsibilities. Leading one of India's largest conglomerates demanded an immense amount of time, energy and focus and his dedication to work often came at the expense of his personal life. Ratan Tata's experiences show how his feelings of loneliness were not unique to him but rather a common struggle for those who prioritize their careers over personal relationships.

Despite the occasional feelings of isolation, Ratan Tata found profound meaning and purpose in his work and philanthropic efforts. In the later years of his life, he became a financial backer of Goodfellows, a start-up that aimed to provide companionship to senior citizens through intergenerational friendships. This was particularly poignant considering his own experiences with solitude. When speaking about the initiative, Tata remarked, 'You don't know what it is to be lonely until you spend time alone wishing for companionship.'

Mentorship and Surrogate Family

In the absence of a traditional family structure, Ratan Tata found fulfilment in mentoring young entrepreneurs and fostering close relationships with colleagues. His bond with Shantanu Naidu, a young entrepreneur who became Tata's business assistant and close friend, is a prime example of how Tata created meaningful connections outside of marriage.

Naidu, in his book *I Came Upon a Lighthouse*, describes his relationship with Ratan Tata as life-changing. This mentorship and friendship provided Ratan with a sense of family and purpose in his later years, demonstrating that meaningful relationships can take many forms.

Legacy and Reflection

As Ratan Tata approached his later years, his perspective on his life choices seemed to soften. In the past, he had openly acknowledged the moments of loneliness he experienced. In his final years, he gained an appreciation for the unique position his bachelorhood afforded him.

Tata's personal story, or whatever is known of it, challenges conventional notions of success and fulfilment wherein marriage and children are viewed as accomplishments rather than just life events that some people choose to forego. It is a testament to the fact that a life without a traditional family structure can still be rich with purpose, achievement and a positive impact on society.

Ratan Tata Quotes

One day you will realise that material things mean nothing. All that matters is the well-being of the people you love.

Ratan Tata: His Life and Work II

2000	Andhra Valley Power Supply Co., and Tata Hydro-Electric Power Supply Company merge into Tata Power to create India's biggest power utility in the private sector.
2000	Tata Group exits cement business; sells its remaining stake in Ambuja Cement to the Gujarat Ambuja Cements Group.
2000	Tata Tea (now Tata Consumer Products) acquires Britain's Tetley for $432 million in a leveraged buyout; becomes the world's second-largest branded tea company.
2000	Ratan Tata receives the Padma Bhushan, India's third-highest civilian honour.
2002	Tata Sons acquires majority stake in government-owned Videsh Sanchar Nigam Ltd (now Tata Communications) for ₹2,599 crore.
2004	Tata Motors gets listed on the New York Stock Exchange.
2004	Indian Hotels Company forays into the value hospitality segment; opens its first Ginger Hotel in Bengaluru.
2004	TCS gets listed on the Bombay Stock Exchange (BSE) and the National Stock Exchange (NSE).
2005	Tata exits Idea Cellular, its joint venture with AV Birla Group and the US-based AT&T, to focus on CDMA-based mobile telephony business.
2006	The Group enters the direct-to-home (DTH) broadcasting space by launching Tata Sky.
2007	Tata Steel acquires Corus (now Tata Steel Europe) for $12.2 billion to become the world's fifth-biggest steel maker.
2008	Tata Motors acquires Jaguar Land Rover from Ford Motor Co., for $2.23 billion.
2008	Tata Motors launches Tata Nano, the world's most affordable car.
2008	Ratan Tata is awarded the Padma Vibhushan, the country's second-highest civilian honour.
26 November 2008	Terrorists storm Indian Hotels-run Taj Mahal Palace in Mumbai.
2010	Ratan Tata files a petition in the Supreme Court on the Niira Radia tape leak incident, saying it violated his privacy; argues that the tapped conversations were leaked to the media because of corporate rivalry.
2012	Tata Global Beverage (now Tata Consumer Products) signs a JV with Starbucks to launch Starbucks cafés in India.

Continued ...

CHAPTER 7

RETIREMENT AND CONTINUING INFLUENCE

- Stepping Down as Chairman
- Legacy and Future Leadership at Tata Group
- Post-retirement Ventures

Stepping Down as Chairman

Ratan Tata's tenure as chairman of Tata Sons, spanning over two decades from 1991 to 2012, was characterized by extraordinary levels of growth and global expansion for the Tata Group.

Preparing for Succession

As Ratan Tata approached his seventies, the question of succession became increasingly pressing for the Tata Group. The final years of his chairmanship involved careful planning, strategic decisions and a commitment to ensuring a smooth transition that would preserve the Group's values and future objectives.

In 2005, a significant decision was made – Tata Sons, the

holding company of the Tata Group, raised the retirement age for non-executive directors from 70 to 75 years. This move allowed Ratan Tata to extend his chairmanship until 2012, providing the necessary additional time he wanted to identify and groom a suitable successor. The decision was seen as a strategic manoeuvre to ensure stability at a time when the global economy was subject to uncertainties and change.

During these extended years, Tata focused on consolidating the Group's achievements and preparing it for future challenges. The succession planning process was thorough and discreet. In August 2010, Tata Sons formed a five-member selection committee to choose the next chairman. This committee, comprising both Tata Group veterans and external advisers, was tasked with the crucial responsibility of identifying a leader who could steer the conglomerate through the complexities of the twenty-first century while upholding its core values.

Within this context, Tata not only wanted to select his own successor but also wanted to cultivate leadership across the group. Under his guidance, the Tata Group implemented comprehensive succession planning processes at various levels and in several companies. The successful transitions completed in listed Tata companies during the last two decades of his tenure were impressive and included key positions at Titan, Voltas, Rallis and Indian Hotels. In 2011, as part of this process, the Tata Group once again adjusted its retirement policies. The retirement age for non-executive directors was brought back down to seventy years. This change was perceived as a way to 'shuffle the deck' and bring younger leaders to the forefront. However, to manage the transition smoothly, directors who had already crossed seventy were allowed to continue until seventy-five.

During this period, Ratan Tata remained committed to the group's ethical standards and social responsibilities. While the search for his successor progressed, he was also actively involved in preparing the group for the transition. Ratan worked on strengthening the group's corporate centre, enhancing coordination between different Tata companies and reinforcing the shared values that bound the diverse businesses together.

Choosing Cyrus Mistry

The culmination of this careful planning came in November 2011 when Cyrus Mistry was officially announced as Ratan Tata's successor. Mistry, who had been on the board of Tata Sons since August 2006 and had long-standing family ties with the group, initially served on the committee tasked with finding Ratan Tata's replacement. During the selection process, Mistry's contributions and insights impressed the committee members to such an extent that they decided to consider him as a candidate himself. In October 2010, Mistry was asked to present his vision for the Tata Group via email due to health reasons that prevented his in-person attendance. His response demonstrated a comprehensive understanding of the Group's challenges and future directions. He proposed a six-year tenure for the chairman to effect meaningful change, suggested modifications to the articles of association of Tata operating companies and envisioned the incubation of four major businesses over five years.

Ratan Tata was particularly impressed by Mistry's performance on the board, noting his 'astute observations and his humility'. Mistry's qualifications were further bolstered by his entrepreneurial background, familiarity with the group as a board member and his family's significant 18 per cent stake in Tata Sons. Tata endorsed Mistry enthusiastically and committed his remaining year to working closely with him and providing the necessary exposure and experience, while Mistry served as 'chairman designate'. Tata described the appointment as 'a good and farsighted choice' and expressed confidence in Mistry's ability to lead the group.

As he approached his final days as chairman, Ratan Tata reflected on the journey of the group under his leadership. This largely India-centric conglomerate had been transformed into a global powerhouse with a presence in over a hundred countries. The group's revenue had grown from $5.8 billion in 1991 to $83.3 billion in 2011. More than the financial growth, Tata took pride in how the group had maintained its ethical standards throughout this expansion.

Transition Period and Handover

In the year leading up to Ratan Tata's retirement, he worked closely with Mistry to familiarize him with the intricacies of the group's operations and its long-term strategic vision. Ratan used this period to reflect on his tenure and the future of the group. As his retirement date approached, he oversaw the completion of several ongoing projects and initiatives, determined to leave the group in a strong position for Mistry.

On 28 December 2012, Ratan Tata officially stepped down as chairman of Tata Sons, signalling the end of an era for the Tata Group. The handover ceremony was a low-key affair, in keeping with Tata's modest style. Cyrus Mistry assumed the role of chairman, becoming only the sixth chairman in the group's 150-year history and the second from outside the Tata family.

In his parting message to employees, Ratan Tata emphasized the importance of continuity, stating, 'I feel confident that the robust growth that India has shown over the past several years will be re-established and the strong fundamentals in the country will result in India once again taking its place as one of the economic success stories of the region.'

Legacy and Future Leadership at Tata Group

After his retirement, Ratan Tata's association with the Tata Group continued as he provided strategic guidance to his successor. Upon his retirement, Ratan was appointed chairman emeritus of Tata Sons, a role that allowed him to maintain a connection with the group he had led for over two decades. This position was not merely honorary; it also enabled Ratan Tata to offer his vast experience and insights to the group's leadership.

One of Ratan Tata's most significant post-retirement roles was his continued leadership of the Tata Trusts, which control 66 per cent of Tata Sons. This position ensured that he remained a key decision-maker in the group's overall direction. Under his port-retirement stewardship, the trusts intensified their social development efforts.

Ratan Tata emerged as a prominent figure in India's burgeoning start-up ecosystem after his retirement. He made several personal investments in 46 start-ups, including well-known names such as Ola, Snapdeal and Paytm. He became a mentor and adviser to many of the young entrepreneurs leading these companies.

The Tata Trusts, under Ratan Tata's guidance post-retirement, initiated several groundbreaking projects in healthcare, education and rural development. One notable example was the establishment of the Tata Medical Center in Kolkata. He also extended his support for numerous academic initiatives. The Tata Trusts provided a grant of ₹75 crore to the Centre for Neuroscience at the Indian Institute of Science to study mechanisms underlying the cause of Alzheimer's disease and to evolve methods for its early diagnosis and treatment. This grant was, spread over five years, beginning in 2014. Furthermore, Tata continued to be a vocal advocate for corporate social responsibility, and he made significant contributions to disaster relief efforts. As a mentor, Tata frequently engaged with young leaders and entrepreneurs, sharing his immense wisdom accumulated during his decades of experience.

On 24 October 2016, the board of directors of Tata Sons voted to remove Cyrus Mistry from his position as chairman, less than four years into his tenure. This decision created ripples throughout corporate India and resulted in a high-profile boardroom battle.

Cyrus Mistry

Mistry was summoned to a board meeting at Bombay House, the headquarters of the Tata Group. To his surprise, he was confronted by his predecessor, Ratan Tata, and board member Nitin Nohria, who informed Mistry that the relationship between him and Ratan Tata 'had not been working' and that the Tata Trusts had decided to move a board resolution for his removal. Mistry was given the option to either resign or face the resolution at the upcoming board meeting. When he chose not to resign, the board convened and voted on his removal. Out of the nine board members, six voted in favour of Mistry's ouster, while two abstained. The decision was swift and final, leaving Mistry with no choice but to vacate the position he had held since 2012.

While the official statement from Tata Sons cited the long-term interests of Tata Sons and Tata Group as the reason for Mistry's removal, various factors were speculated to have contributed to this drastic action. These included divergent management styles, performance concerns, strategic disagreements and governance issues. Mistry's approach to managing the conglomerate reportedly clashed with Tata's time-honoured way of doing business, and there was dissatisfaction with the financial performance of certain Tata Group companies under Mistry's leadership. His decisions to divest certain assets and focus on cash-generating businesses were said to have caused friction with the old guard. Later, Tata Sons alleged that Mistry had misled the selection committee in 2011 by making 'lofty statements' about his plans for the group, which were ultimately not implemented.

In the wake of Mistry's removal, Ratan Tata stepped back into an active role as the interim chairman of Tata Sons. This was done as a stabilizing measure to reassure stakeholders and guide the group through the crisis. Ratan's immediate actions upon return included addressing group CEOs, emphasizing that it was 'business as usual' and urging them to focus on their respective businesses. He disbanded Mistry's six-member strategy team, signalling a shift in management approach. He also initiated the search for a new chairman by forming a selection committee to identify a permanent successor within four months.

Mistry's removal sparked a protracted legal battle that would last years. Mistry criticized the decision and alleged that he had not been given the freedom to effectively manage the conglomerate. The Shapoorji Pallonji Group, which held an 18.4 per cent stake in Tata Sons through Mistry's family, challenged the ouster in various legal forums. The dispute reached the National Company Law Appellate Tribunal (NCLAT), which in December 2019 ordered Mistry's reinstatement as executive chairman. However, this decision was ultimately overturned by the Supreme Court in 2021, bringing an end to the long-running legal saga.

The sudden move had immediate repercussions for the Tata Group. The shares of most of the listed Tata companies fell in the immediate aftermath of Mistry's removal, reflecting investor uncertainty. The public dispute between Mistry and Tata Sons raised questions about the group's governance and decision-making processes. Moreover, some of Mistry's decisions and initiatives were re-evaluated under the interim leadership of Ratan Tata.

On 12 January 2017, N. Chandrasekaran became the new chairman of Tata Sons after a selection process in which he was personally hand-picked by Ratan Tata. Chandrasekaran had joined Tata Consultancy Services (TCS) in 1987 as an intern and steadily rose through the ranks over three decades. His performance as the CEO of TCS since 2009 had been exemplary as he had successfully helped the company evolve into India's most valuable firm and a global IT powerhouse. Under his leadership, TCS saw its revenue jump three-fold from ₹30,000 crore in 2010 to ₹1.09 lakh crore in 2016, indicating his impressive record that contributed majorly to his selection.

After Mistry's ouster, a five-member selection committee was formed to identify the right candidate. Chandrasekaran's status as a Tata Group insider played a crucial role in his selection. Having spent his entire career with the group, he was deeply familiar with its culture, values and operations, which was seen by Ratan Tata as vital for maintaining continuity and stability. Chandrasekaran's appointment was also viewed as a strategic move to bring a fresh perspective to the Group's leadership. As the first non-Parsi and first professional executive to head the Tata Group, his selection represented a significant departure from previous chairman appointments. His extensive experience in the technology sector was another factor that worked in his favour. Known for his ability to take calculated risks and make tough business decisions, he had demonstrated his capacity to disrupt established norms for the better. For instance, his decision to break TCS into 23 units for smoother service delivery and operations was later adopted by other IT giants such as Infosys.

The board of Tata Sons, in announcing Chandrasekaran's appointment, highlighted his exemplary leadership at TCS and expressed confidence in his ability to inspire the entire Tata Group. Due to his enviable reputation, his appointment as chairman helped restore confidence in the Tata Group following the public dispute with Mistry.

The transition process was carefully managed. Chandrasekaran was appointed as a director on the board of Tata Sons on 25 October 2016, a day after Mistry was ousted. He officially assumed the role of executive chairman on 21 February 2017, following a unanimous recommendation by the selection committee. This move was also well-received by the business community and Tata Group stakeholders.

In the years following his appointment, Chandrasekaran has focused on implementing his 'One Tata' strategy, which highlights simplification, synergy and scale across the group's diverse businesses. He has successfully steered the group towards new ventures in areas like semiconductors, electronics manufacturing and battery technology.

As Ratan Tata approached his later years, his legacy was crucial in providing guidance to N. Chandrasekaran. The latter aptly summarized Tata's enduring impact, stating, 'Mr Tata's dedication to philanthropy and the development of society has touched the lives of millions. From education to healthcare, his initiatives have left a deep-rooted mark that will benefit generations to come. Reinforcing all of this work was Mr. Tata's genuine humility in every individual interaction.' He further added that the Tata Group under Ratan Tata's stewardship had greatly expanded its global footprint while remaining true to its moral compass.

As the dust settled on the leadership controversy, Ratan Tata continued to be a respected figure in Indian business and philanthropy. His retirement, despite the subsequent challenges, was seen as a model of planned succession in Indian corporate history.

Post-retirement Ventures

After stepping down as chairman of Tata Sons in 2012, Ratan Tata embarked on a new chapter in his life. Far from retreating into quiet retirement, he remained an active and influential figure in India's business landscape. His venture into start-up investments was, by his own admission, somewhat accidental. In a 2019 interaction, he recalled, 'I entered the start-up investor partly by accident. During the years that I was with the Tata Group, I always looked at the start-ups as a sector that is exciting but somewhat untouchable because somewhere there will be conflict of interest with Tata Group.' Despite this initial hesitation, Ratan Tata went on to invest in forty-six Indian start-ups in his lifetime, of which nine became unicorns, five were listed and three were acquired.

Some of his notable investments

1. Ola and Ola Electric

Ratan Tata had first invested in ANI Technologies, Ola's parent company, in acknowledgement of the ride-hailing platform's disruptive potential in India's transportation sector. In May 2019, Tata decided to extend his support to Ola Electric Mobility Pvt Ltd as part of his Series A funding round. This investment came at a juncture when the company was developing solutions to make electric mobility viable at a large scale in the country. Tata's decision to invest was driven by his belief in the evolving electric vehicle ecosystem and Ola Electric's potential to play a key role in its growth.

Bhavish Aggarwal, co-founder & CEO of Ola, admitted that Ratan Tata had a significant influence on him by being a great source of inspiration, as well as a personal mentor. The impact of Ratan Tata's investment and guidance has been substantial. His endorsement lent credibility to Ola Electric's approach in developing an electric mobility ecosystem, including innovations in charging infrastructure and swapping models. The company has since made significant strides, such as in running pilot projects aimed at effective charging solutions, battery-swapping stations and deploying vehicles across various segments.

Tata's support also helped Ola Electric attract further investments and partnerships, including a significant deal with Hyundai and Kia. These collaborations accelerated Ola's progress in becoming a 'Smart Mobility Solutions Provider' and developing India-specific electric vehicle infrastructure.

2. Paytm

Ratan Tata's investment in Paytm in 2015 was his fifth personal investment in India's burgeoning digital economy. This move demonstrated Tata's foresight regarding the potential of mobile payments and digital commerce in transforming India's financial sector. His decision to invest in Paytm was influenced by several factors. He was impressed by the visionary leadership of Vijay Shekhar Sharma, Paytm's founder, along with his ambition to build a cashless economy in India. Ratan Tata understood the enormous market potential in India's largely unbanked and underbanked population and was aware that a platform like Paytm could democratize access to financial services.

The timing of Tata's investment occurred before India's demonetization in 2016, which later accelerated the adoption of digital payments. He took on an advisory role at Paytm, bringing his wisdom to guide the company's growth. Vijay Shekhar Sharma expressed his appreciation, stating, 'I'm happy that someone like him (Tata) has put his faith and trust in our values and mission. There is no better adviser for Paytm on building India's most trusted payment and commerce platform.'

Tata's endorsement of Paytm lent credibility to the platform and helped it attract more users and further investments. Under Tata's guidance, Paytm expanded its services beyond digital payments and became a comprehensive financial platform by including e-commerce, banking and insurance services. Tata's involvement also helped Paytm navigate regulatory challenges and build trust with consumers and regulators alike.

3. Snapdeal

Ratan Tata's investment in Snapdeal in August 2014 marked his entry into the e-commerce landscape. He secured a 0.17 per cent stake, making an initial investment of less than ₹5 crore. When this investment was made, India was still in its nascent stages in terms of e-commerce, and billion-dollar valuations were rare. Ratan Tata's investment also coincided with Flipkart's acquisition of Myntra, and his decision to back Snapdeal helped maintain a competitive landscape in the e-commerce sector.

Ratan Tata's investment in Snapdeal lent considerable credibility to the platform, and the company quickly succeeded in establishing itself as a formidable e-commerce platform that could challenge industry giants like Amazon and Flipkart. As a mentor, he spent time in engaging with Snapdeal's leadership, providing strategic advice and insights drawn from his extensive experience. Even when Snapdeal faced significant challenges in subsequent years, including intense competition and changing market dynamics, Ratan Tata remained steadfast in his support. He continued to provide strategic counsel, which helped the company overcome several obstacles.

4. Urban Company

Ratan Tata invested in Urban Company, formerly known as UrbanClap, in December 2015 by committing an undisclosed amount to the company, which was at the time a budding marketplace for local services like plumbing, electrical work and beauty treatments. The company's vision of providing reliable, high-quality services to urban consumers while creating employment opportunities for service professionals resonated well with Ratan Tata's philosophy of supporting businesses that contribute to societal progress.

Ratan's involvement provided the start-up with invaluable visibility in the market. Abhiraj Singh Bhal, co-founder of Urban Company, recounted his first meeting with Tata, who had assured Bhal that 'India needs what you are building.' With Ratan Tata's mentorship, Bhal was able to rapidly expand Urban Company by refining its service offerings, improving its technology platform and commencing services in multiple cities across India. Ratan Tata's backing proved to be effective in instilling confidence in other investors, as well as potential employees. The company's success under Ratan Tata's guidance is evident in its growth trajectory: from a local services marketplace, it has now evolved into a comprehensive platform offering a wide range of professional services across multiple cities. By 2024, Urban Company had become a prominent name in India's service industry.

5. FirstCry

FirstCry was started as an e-commerce platform specializing in baby and kids' products. In 2016, Ratan Tata made a personal investment in this company due to its unique positioning in a previously untapped market segment. The platform's focus on providing a wide range of high-quality baby and mother care products greatly impressed Tata. His backing resulted in enhancing FirstCry's reputation in the market for consumers and other investors alike. Supam Maheshwari, FirstCry's founder and CEO, highlighted the significance of Ratan Tata's involvement, stating, 'A positive nod from a business leader of Tata's stature is a great vote of confidence in the way we have created the ecosystem and validation of the business approach leading to a definitive path to profitability.'

Under Ratan Tata's mentorship, FirstCry expanded its product range and improved its logistics network, which consequently strengthened its market position. Tata's investment also proved to be financially rewarding – as FirstCry prepared for its IPO in 2023, Ratan Tata was set to divest all 77,900 shares he held in the company, amounting to a 0.02 per cent stake. At the IPO price of ₹465 per share, Ratan Tata's stake was valued at approximately ₹3.62 crore, representing a 449 per cent return on his initial investment. However, on the day of the listing, FirstCry's shares opened at ₹651 on NSE, indicating a 40 per cent premium over the issue price. At this price, Ratan Tata's stake was valued at ₹5.07 crore, delivering him a return of 670 per cent.

6. Lenskart

Lenskart is a leading online eyewear retailer with a presence in multiple Indian cities. In April 2016, Ratan Tata invested a modest sum of ₹10 lakh in Lenskart, with the impact of his involvement far exceeding the financial contribution. Tata's decision to invest in Lenskart was likely driven by the company's innovative approach to disrupting the traditional eyewear market. Despite having his own eyewear brand, Titan EyePlus, Ratan recognized the potential in Lenskart's digital-first model and its ability to make quality and fashionable eyewear even more accessible.

While Ratan Tata's financial contribution was relatively small, he mentored the company towards remarkable growth through the strengthening of its online presence, expansion of its product range and development of an innovative omnichannel approach by establishing physical stores alongside the digital platform.

The success of Lenskart through the direct influence of Ratan Tata is clearly demonstrated in its impressive valuation growth. By 2024, Lenskart had achieved a valuation of $5 billion. Moreover, Ratan Tata's investment yielded substantial returns for him, reportedly yielding a return 28 times his initial investment.

7. CureFit

In 2017, Ratan Tata invested $3 million in CureFit, a health and fitness start-up, through his UC RNT Fund. This investment was part of a larger $18 million funding round, making CureFit one of the most well-funded early-stage start-ups in India at the time. The company's holistic approach to health and wellness was appreciated by Ratan Tata. CureFit's multifaceted platform, which includes fitness centres (Cult.fit), food delivery (Eat.fit), healthcare clinics (Care.fit) and mental wellness services (Mind.fit), were likely contributors to Ratan Tata's decision to financially back the business.

Ratan Tata's initial investment in CureFit paved the way for larger investments. Specifically, in 2021, Tata Digital, which was a subsidiary of Tata Sons, invested $75 million in CureFit, further accelerating the company's expansion plans. The company was thereafter able to refine its service offerings and expand its presence across multiple cities in India. Today, CureFit has evolved from a fitness start-up to a comprehensive health and wellness platform, as well as a leading player in India's health and fitness industry.

CHAPTER 8

RATAN TATA'S GLOBAL LEGACY

- Impact on Indian Industry and Economy
- Legacy of Industrial and Global Leadership
- Global Recognition and Honours
-

Impact on Indian Industry and Economy

The impact of the Tata Group's Ratan-Tata years - from 1991 to 2012 - can be seen today on both the conglomerate and India's industrial landscape. The beginning of his tenure coincided with the liberalization of the Indian economy, and Tata's farsightedness helped the Group capitalize on the emergence of unforeseen markets. The Tata Group underwent significant restructuring and consolidation during his chairmanship, guided by his focus on innovation, quality and global competitiveness, expanding the group's portfolio into new industries like IT and telecommunications, resulting in enormous financial growth.

Strategic acquisitions, such as Tetley, Corus Steel and Jaguar Land Rover, were the highlights of Ratan Tata's career. These moves not only expanded Tata's international footprint but also showcased Indian companies on the world stage.

His leadership style prioritized ethical business practices, corporate social responsibility and sustainable development. Ratan Tata integrated CSR into the group's business strategy and focused on nurturing talent and fostering a culture of mentorship.

Ratan Tata's vision extended beyond profit-making to creating impactful, socially responsible businesses. He championed affordable innovation, exemplified by projects like the Tata Nano, aiming to make quality products accessible to the masses, which has had a lasting influence on shaping the nation's business scene and global presence. Under his guidance, companies like TCS and Tata Motors became global leaders in their respective sectors and began contributing significantly to India's economic growth. Therefore, it is not an exaggeration to say that Ratan's legacy has influenced seasoned businessmen and new entrepreneurs alike through the benchmarks it has set for ethical leadership, innovation and global expansion.

Ratan Tata drafted the Tata Group's strategic plan in 1983, which set the Group on a course of expansion and impact through significant contributions such as the Tata Group's journey into becoming a global powerhouse. Under his leadership, the Group's revenue grew over forty times, and profits increased over fifty times.

This transformation was achieved through a series of strategic acquisitions and expansions, the most notable of which are Tetley Tea (2000), the world's second-largest branded tea company; Corus Steel (2007), among the world's largest steel producers; and the luxury-segment Jaguar Land Rover (2008). These acquisitions had a large role in India's entry into the international market and demonstrated the ability of Indian businesses to compete on a global stage. As he himself stated, 'What we did was to create a foundation for the future. I think we will be judged by the quality of what we did, not the volume.'

Ratan Tata's aim to create groundbreaking products that would be also affordable for the average person was trailblazing. Regardless of its failure, Tata Nano remains the most notable example of this approach. Moreover, Tata deftly guided the group as it entered the telecommunications sector with Tata Teleservices in 1996, and his foresight paid off in this sector.

Ratan Tata played a crucial role in establishing India as a global IT powerhouse. His leadership saw the growth of TCS into one of the world's largest IT services companies. The decision to list TCS on the stock market in 2004 was a landmark moment that paved the way for other Indian IT companies to gain international recognition.

Ratan Tata's focus on R&D helped position Indian companies as innovators rather than just service providers. His focus on research played a huge hand in changing the Indian automotive industry through the development of the Tata Indica – India's first indigenously designed and manufactured passenger car and a milestone in the country's automotive history. This was followed by the ambitious Nano project, which, despite its commercial failure, was boundary-pushing in terms of cost-effective engineering and manufacturing.

In 2007, the acquisition of Corus Steel was a defining moment for both Tata Steel and the Indian steel industry. This $12 billion deal was one of the largest acquisitions ever made by an Indian company at the time. It catapulted Tata Steel to be among the world's top steel producers by revenue.

Ratan Tata also exhibited exemplary leadership with his prioritization of ethical business practices under social responsibility initiatives and investments in start-ups after his retirement as chairman. He invested in 46 start-ups, many of which can now be considered successful ventures, including Ola, Paytm and Lenskart. His involvement in the start-up ecosystem, encompassing his mentorship and guidance apart from financial assistance, benefited several entrepreneurs.

Legacy of Global Leadership

Ratan Tata's influence in the business world extended far beyond the borders of India; it left an indelible mark on leaders across various professions across the world. His approach to business leadership resonated with many international corporate figures and the way he helped the Tata Group evolve into an international conglomerate while maintaining its ethical foundation is widely admired.

Carlos Ghosn, former CEO of Renault-Nissan Alliance, has publicly stated that he was inspired by the Tata Nano to launch Renault Kwid. He said, 'I was the first one, maybe the only one, to say he (Ratan Tata) was a visionary on launching the Nano.' Giving credit to the path paved by Ratan Tata for the success of Renault Kwid, he admitted, 'We followed and I am glad we followed the Nano because the success of Renault today in India is mainly based on the success of the Kwid.'

In the realm of philanthropy, Ratan Tata's frequent prioritization of sustainable development has left a lasting impact. The Tata Trusts, under his guidance, have consistently supported projects related to education, healthcare and rural development.

Bill Gates characterized Ratan Tata as a forward-thinking individual whose impact extended far and wide. Gates noted the profound and lasting influence he had in both his home country and the global community. Reflecting on their collaborative efforts, he stated, 'Together, we partnered on numerous initiatives to help people lead healthier, more prosperous lives.' The Microsoft co-founder expressed his belief that Ratan Tata's legacy would serve as a source of inspiration for generations to come, highlighting the enduring nature of his contributions.

Ratan Tata's philanthropic efforts outside India included his donation of $50 million to his alma mater, Harvard Business School, for the establishment of an executive centre. He also established a $28 million Tata Scholarship Fund at Cornell University to provide financial aid to promising undergraduate students from India. Within India, he awarded a grant of ₹750 million in 2014 to the Centre for Neuroscience at the Indian Institute of Science to investigate the causes of Alzheimer's disease and improve early diagnosis and treatment. During the Covid-19 pandemic, he directed the Tata Trusts to contribute $270 million towards relief efforts.

> Ratan Tata's friendship with Shantanu Naidu is a heartwarming tale of inter-generational bonding that defies conventions. Their connection began in 2014 when Naidu, a fifth-generation Tata employee, reached out to Ratan Tata seeking support for his initiative to protect stray dogs. Naidu's project, which involved creating glow-in-the-dark collars for dogs to prevent road accidents, resonated with Ratan's lifelong love

of animals. Impressed by Naidu's compassion and innovation, Ratan Tata invited him to Mumbai, marking the beginning of their unique relationship. Their shared passion for animal welfare led to the launch of Motopaws, a venture dedicated to reducing animal-related accidents. As their bond deepened, Naidu affectionately dubbed Ratan Tata 'Millennial Dumbledore', highlighting the industrialist's wisdom and spirit. Their friendship transcended professional boundaries, with the duo enjoying activities like watching action–comedy films and getting haircuts together. Ratan Tata's mentorship of Naidu went beyond business as he supported Naidu's pursuit of an MBA in the United States and also attended his graduation. Upon Naidu's return, he became Ratan Tata's assistant and the youngest manager of the Tata Trusts, further solidifying their connection. Their relationship also inspired Naidu to launch Goodfellows, a start-up connecting young people with senior citizens for companionship. Throughout their friendship, Ratan Tata genuinely cared for Naidu, even buying him a replacement shirt when his original one tore. This gesture exemplifies the depth of their bond, which Naidu describes as a mix of personal and professional. Their friendship, which flourished despite the significant age gap, has shown that meaningful connections can be fostered regardless of generational differences.

Final Days

As Ratan Tata entered his mid-eighties, he began to suffer from health challenges typical of advanced age. In early October 2024, concerns about his health began to circulate when he was admitted to Mumbai's Breach Candy Hospital. On 7 October 2024, he made his final public communication through an Instagram post:

> I am aware of recent rumours circulating regarding my health and want to assure everyone that these claims are unfounded. I am currently undergoing medical check-ups due to my age and related medical conditions. There is no cause for concern. I remain in good spirits and request that the public and media refrain from spreading misinformation.

However, contrary to his reassurance, Ratan Tata's condition deteriorated rapidly in the subsequent days. On 9 October 2024 at 11:30 p.m. IST, Ratan Naval Tata passed away at the age of 86. The news of his death sent shockwaves considering his last public message, and his death marked the end of an era in India's industrial evolution history.

The passing of Ratan Tata elicited an outpouring of grief and tributes from public figures across India and the world. Prime Minister Narendra Modi led the nation in mourning, describing Ratan Tata as 'a visionary business leader, a compassionate soul and an extraordinary human being' who 'endeared himself to several people thanks to his humility, kindness and an unwavering commitment to making our society better'. This sentiment was echoed by leaders from various fields, all acknowledging Tata's immense contributions.

In recognition of his stature and contributions, the Government of Maharashtra and the Government of Jharkhand announced a day of mourning. On 10 October 2024, Ratan Tata was accorded a state funeral – a rare honour that reflected his iconic status. His last rites were conducted at the Parsi crematorium in Worli, Mumbai. He was given full military honours, including a 21-gun salute. The Mumbai Police provided a ceremonial guard of honour, and his body was draped in the Indian flag to honour his contributions to the nation. The funeral was attended by the who's who of Indian society, including prominent industrialists, politicians and celebrities. Union Home Minister Amit Shah, Maharashtra Chief Minister Eknath Shinde and Gujarat Chief Minister Bhupendra Patel were among the dignitaries present to pay their last respects.

Ratan Tata's philanthropic nature outshone his other traits. It was revealed that in his will, Tata had bequeathed ₹10,000 crore (approximately $1.2 billion) to various charitable causes.

In the days following Ratan Tata's passing, personal anecdotes and tributes poured in from those who had known him. Shantanu Naidu, his long-time friend, shared a poignant farewell on social media, referring to Ratan Tata as his 'lighthouse'. Cricket legend Sachin Tendulkar, one of the first to arrive at Tata's residence after the news broke, shared his thoughts on social media:

> In his life, and demise, Mr Ratan Tata has moved the nation. I was fortunate to spend time with him, but millions, who have never met him, feel the same grief that I feel today. Such is his impact. From his love for animals to philanthropy, he showed that true progress can only be achieved when we care for those who don't have the means to take care of themselves.

Rohit Sharma, another prominent cricketer, expressed that Ratan Tata 'will forever be remembered as someone who truly cared and lived his life to make everyone else's better'.

In his final years, there had been discussions about Ratan Tata penning his autobiography. N.K. Singh, chairman of the 15th Finance Commission, recalled a conversation with him on this subject:

> When I asked him about his autobiography, Ratan replied with characteristic humility. He said he had not written one, but a biography had been compiled which he had thrown out of the window, adding that it was meaningless to add to the gossip and anecdotes of Mumbai's Willingdon Club. He then asked me what his autobiography might say and if it would serve any public purpose. I responded that he had seen pre-Independence India, a newly independent India with its struggles for food and foreign exchange in an over-regulated economy, and was part of the country's subsequent growth story, which is now unfolding into a quest to become a developed economy by 2047.

He added further, 'Legends like Ratan Tata live on forever. Few lives embody the essence of service like his. I had the honour of knowing and working with him, and his humility and vision never ceased to amaze me.'

As the world bids farewell to Ratan Tata, there was a collective reflection on the values he embodied and the legacy he left behind. His life story – from a young man who nearly settled down in Los Angeles to becoming a titanic figure in India's business world – will continue to serve as an inspiration to generations of Indians. His life also illustrates the key belief that business is not just about making money, it is also about being responsible, adventurous and generous. He showed us how to adapt to changes in a fast-paced world of technology.

In the end, Ratan's life and legacy is a remarkable example of how a single individual, driven by dedication, integrity and compassion for others, can leave a memorable mark on society. As India forges ahead on its path of economic and social advancements, the ethical principles and core values that Ratan Tata embodied throughout his life continue to live on.

Recognition and Honours

Indian National Honours

Ratan Tata received several of India's highest civilian honours in recognition of his contributions to industry and society. In 2000, he was awarded the Padma Bhushan, the third-highest civilian award in India. This was followed in 2008 by the Padma Vibhushan, the second-highest civilian honour in the country. These awards underscore the immense respect Ratan Tata commanded within India for his leadership of the Tata Group and his philanthropic endeavours.

In addition to these national honours, Tata also received recognition from various Indian states. In 2006, he was conferred with the Maharashtra Bhushan, the highest civilian award in the state of Maharashtra. In 2021, he received the Assam Baibhav award, specifically for his contributions to cancer care in Assam. Most recently, in 2023, Tata became the first recipient of the newly instituted Maharashtra Udyog Ratna award, created by the Government of Maharashtra on the lines of the Maharashtra Bhushan to recognize outstanding contributions in the field of business.

International Governmental Honours

Here is a list of some prominent international awards Ratan Tata received from different countries:

United Kingdom: In 2009, Ratan Tata was honoured as an Honorary Knight Commander of the Order of the British Empire (KBE) by Queen Elizabeth II. This was elevated in 2014 to Honorary Knight Grand Cross of the Order of the British Empire (GBE). The GBE is the highest class of the Order of the British Empire and is a rare honour for non-British citizens. This recognition highlighted Ratan Tata's contributions to trade and investment in the UK.

France: In 2016, the Government of France conferred upon Ratan Tata the title of Commander of the Legion of Honour. This is one of France's highest distinctions, and it recognizes eminent service to France. The award acknowledged Tata's contributions to strengthening economic ties between France and India, as well as his leadership in promoting Indo-French cooperation in various sectors.

Japan: In 2012, Ratan Tata received the Grand Cordon of the Order of the Rising Sun from the Government of Japan. This is one of Japan's highest honours for foreign nationals. The award acknowledged Ratan Tata's significant role in strengthening economic relations between Japan and India, particularly through the Tata Group's collaborations with Japanese companies and his efforts in promoting bilateral trade and investment.

Italy: In 2009, Ratan Tata was honoured as a Grand Officer of the Order of Merit of the Italian Republic. This is one of the highest orders of knighthood in Italy. The award appreciated his contributions to strengthening Italian–Indian business relations and his role in promoting economic cooperation between the two countries.

Australia: In 2023, King Charles III conferred upon Ratan Tata the title of Honorary Officer of the Order of Australia. This honour recognizes individuals who have made a significant contribution to Australia or humanity at large. The award acknowledged Ratan Tata's role in nurturing strong economic and cultural bonds between Australia and India in trade, investment and philanthropy.

Uruguay: In 2004, Ratan Tata received the Medal of the Oriental Republic of Uruguay from the government of Uruguay. This award is typically given to foreign nationals who have made significant contributions to Uruguay or to the country's international relations.

Singapore: In 2008, the Government of Singapore awarded Ratan Tata the Honorary Citizen Award. This is the highest form of appreciation for non-Singaporeans and is rarely bestowed. It recognized his role in strengthening economic ties between Singapore and India and his contributions to Singapore's development as a global business hub.

Ratan Tata Quotes

My most visible goal is to do something in nutrition to children in India, and pregnant mothers. Because that would change the mental and physical health of our population in years to come

Academic Honours

Ratan Tata's contributions to business and society were widely known by academic institutions around the world. He received numerous honorary doctorates, including these:

Indian Institutes of Technology (Bombay, Kharagpur, Madras): Ratan Tata received honorary doctor of science degrees from three prestigious Indian Institutes of Technology for his significance in India's technological and industrial evolution. These honours were bestowed between 2006 and 2008 to commemorate his focus on technology and innovation, which aligns closely with the IITs' mission of fostering technical excellence.

University of Cambridge: The conferment of an honorary doctor of law degree by the University of Cambridge in 2010 highlights Ratan Tata's global stature as a business leader. This prestigious honour from one of the world's oldest and most renowned universities was bestowed in appreciation of Ratan Tata's impact on international relations, ethical business practices and social development.

Ohio State University: Ohio State University awarded Ratan Tata with an honorary doctor of business administration in 2001. This honour came at a time when Ratan Tata was actively steering the Tata Group towards international expansion and modernization and acknowledges his innovative approach to business management and his success in tackling globalization challenges for the Tata Group. It was also based on his contributions to management education and his role in fostering India–US business relations.

Carnegie Mellon University: The honorary doctor of business practice by Carnegie Mellon University was awarded to Ratan Tata in 2013. Known for its strong focus on technology and innovation, Carnegie Mellon's recognition illuminates Tata's role in driving technological advancements in areas such as software services (TCS) and automotive innovation (Tata Motors).

Singapore Management University: The Singapore Management University conferred an honorary doctor of business degree on Ratan Tata in 2013 to honour his influence in the Asian business world and his major role in strengthening economic ties between India and other southeast Asian countries.

York University, Canada: York University awarded the honorary doctor of laws degree to Ratan Tata in 2014 in recognition of his global impact beyond the business sphere, in particular, his contributions to international relations and strengthening India–Canada trade ties. The law degree also acknowledges Tata's role in shaping ethical business practices, his advocacy for corporate governance and his philanthropic efforts.

Clemson University: Clemson University conferred an honorary doctorate of automotive engineering in 2015 to Ratan Tata due to his groundbreaking achievements in the automotive industry, as well as for his role in transforming Tata Motors into a global automotive player through the acquisition of Jaguar Land Rover.

Swansea University: The honorary doctorate from Swansea University in 2018 reflects Ratan Tata's longstanding influence on international businesses and educational institutions, as well as his contributions to the UK economy, particularly through the Tata Group's investments in Britain, including the steel sector in Wales.

HSNC University: The honorary doctorate of literature from the Mumbai-based HSNC University in 2022 is a unique recognition of Ratan Tata's multifaceted career and impact on Indian society. The literature degree honoured his role as a thought leader, his articulation of business philosophy and his contributions to the public discourse on social and economic issues in India.

Business and Philanthropy Awards

Ratan Tata's impact on the business world and his philanthropic efforts were acknowledged through numerous awards:

Carnegie Medal of Philanthropy (2007): Ratan Tata was awarded this prestigious medal in 2007 by the Carnegie Endowment for International Peace to honour his significant contributions to various social causes, particularly those related to education, healthcare and rural development. The award is given to individuals who exemplify the philanthropic spirit of Andrew Carnegie, which directly reflects Ratan Tata's commitment to improving the lives of people.

Inspired Leadership Award (2008): Ratan Tata received this award during the Indian Affairs India Leadership Conclave, which recognizes individuals who exemplify exceptional leadership qualities. The award celebrated Tata's transformative impact on the Indian industrial landscape and his dedication to ethical business practices.

Oslo Business for Peace Award (2010): In 2010, Ratan Tata received the Oslo Business for Peace Award from the Business for Peace Foundation, which celebrates ethical business leaders who contribute to peace and prosperity. This award commemorated Tata's commitment to ethical persistence and corporate responsibility throughout his career, as well as his belief that businesses should not only focus on profit but should also work towards societal well-being and sustainable development.

Ernst and Young Entrepreneur of the Year – Lifetime Achievement (2013): Ratan Tata was awarded this for his outstanding contributions to entrepreneurship and business leadership. This accolade highlighted Ratan Tata's transformation of the Tata Group into a global powerhouse and also honoured his ability to inspire future generations of entrepreneurs through innovative thinking.

Lifetime Achievement Award (2014): Ratan Tata was honoured with the Lifetime Achievement Award by the Rockefeller Foundation in 2014 for his extensive philanthropic endeavours. This prestigious award celebrated Tata's unwavering commitment to social causes, particularly through the Tata Trusts.

Sayaji Ratna Award (2014): The Baroda Management Association honoured Ratan Tata with the Sayaji Ratna Award in 2014 for his significant contributions to both Indian industry and society. This is awarded to individuals who have made an enduring impact through their work and philanthropic efforts.

Industry Recognition

Ratan Tata's influence in various industries was acknowledged through specialized honours:

Honorary Fellowship (2008): In 2008, Ratan Tata was awarded an Honorary Fellowship by the Institution of Engineering and Technology (IET), one of the world's largest engineering institutions, in appreciation of his contributions to the fields of engineering and technology.

Foreign Associate of the National Academy of Engineering (2013): In 2013, Ratan Tata was elected as a Foreign Associate of the National Academy of Engineering, a highly selective honour bestowed upon individuals who have made outstanding contributions to engineering research, practice or education.

Transformational Leader of the Decade (2013): Ratan Tata was recognized as the Transformational Leader of the Decade by the Indian Affairs India Leadership Conclave for his enormous role in reshaping the Tata Group, and consequently, the broader Indian industry.

Ratan Tata Quotes

The greatest value that my parents may have given to me was a good education. Don't fritter it away.

I have always been very content with what I do. I am not driven by one-upmanship. I believe that the process of learning never ends.

Ups and downs in life are very important to keep us going, because a straight line even in an ECG means we are not alive.

Ratan Tata: His Life and Work III

December 2012	Ratan Tata steps down as chairman of Tata Sons after five decades with the Tata Group, making way for Cyrus Mistry as the new chairman; the same month he is appointed chairman emeritus of Tata Sons.
2015 onwards	Begins to invest in start-ups.
2016	Mistry is removed as chairman after a legal battle; in March 2021, the Supreme Court rules in favour of Ratan Tata and Tata Sons; says there was no case of oppression and mismanagement against Cyrus Mistry at Tata Sons.
October 2016 February 2017	Ratan serves as interim chairman of Tata Sons.
27 January 2022	Air India returns to the Tata Group after 69 years of being run as a government entity.
April 2022	Ratan Tata delivers his last public address in Assam's Dibrugarh, alongside Prime Minister Modi, at the launch of South Asia's largest network of affordable cancer care hospitals. In his speech, Tata says he has dedicated his 'last years to health (care)'.
7 October 2024	Ratan Tata posts on social media to dismiss speculation surrounding his health, stating that he is undergoing routine medical checkups due to his age.
9 October 2024	Ratan Tata passes away at the age of 86 in Mumbai's Breach Candy Hospital.
10 October 2024	His funeral takes place at Worli crematorium in Mumbai with state honours. Various dignitaries attend the funeral.

CHAPTER 9

REFLECTIONS AND LESSONS

The Tata Code of Conduct

The Tata Code of Conduct (TCOC) was introduced in 1998 by Ratan Tata seven years into his chairmanship, which has since become a cornerstone of the Tata Group's ethical expectations for employees of all levels and business partners.

The TCOC has its roots in the ethical principles that have guided the Tata Group since its inception. However, it was under Ratan Tata's leadership that these principles were codified into a comprehensive document applicable across all Tata companies. Since then the code has undergone several revisions to keep pace with changing business environments and ethical challenges. It was developed through a consultative process involving various stakeholders within the Tata Group, ensuring that it reflected the collective wisdom and values of the organization.

Ratan Tata Quotes

If I had an ideological choice, I would probably want to do something more for the uplift of the people of India. I have a strong desire not to make money but to see happiness created in a place where there isn't.

The TCOC is built on several core principles that form the foundation of ethical behaviour within the group:

- Integrity: It emphasizes the importance of being honest, transparent and ethical in all work-related dealings. This principle extends to financial integrity, requiring accurate and complete financial records and reports.
- Respect for stakeholders: The code underscores respect for all stakeholders, including employees, customers, business partners and the communities in which Tata companies operate. This includes principles of non-discrimination, fair treatment and respect for human rights.
- Excellence: The Tata Group's commitment to excellence is reflected in the code, which encourages employees to strive for the highest standards of quality in their work and to improve their skills and knowledge continuously.
- Unity: It promotes a sense of unity and teamwork across the diverse companies that make up the Tata Group. It encourages collaboration and the sharing of knowledge and resources for the benefit of the entire Group.
- Responsibility: The code stresses the responsibility of Tata companies and employees to act as good corporate citizens, including environmental stewardship and contribution to community development.
- Understanding: This code requires all stakeholders and employees to show care, respect, compassion and humanity towards everyone involved in the Tata Group's companies.

The document also covers several key areas of business ethics and conduct:

- **Human rights:** The Code of Conduct strictly prohibits child labour and any form of slavery. The company respects human rights by not confiscating employees' personal documents, requiring payments for employment and upholding the dignity and rights of all employees.

- **National interest:** The code emphasizes the importance of contributing to national economic development and avoiding any actions that could adversely affect national interests.

- **Financial reporting and records:** It outlines the principles for maintaining accurate financial records and ensuring transparency in financial reporting.

- **Competition:** It provides guidelines for fair competition and prohibits anti-competitive practices.

- **Equal opportunity employer:** It reinforces the Tata Group's commitment to being an equal opportunity employer and prohibits discrimination based on race, caste, religion, colour, ancestry, marital status, gender, sexual orientation, age, nationality, ethnic origin or disability.

- **Gifts and donations:** The code provides guidelines on the acceptance and giving of gifts and donations to ensure that they do not influence business decisions.

- **Government agencies:** It outlines principles for dealing with government agencies, stressing transparency and compliance with all applicable laws and regulations.

- **Political non-alignment:** The code underscores the group's political non-alignment while respecting employees' rights to their personal political views and activities.
- **Health, safety and environment:** It underscores the group's commitment to providing a safe and healthy working environment, as well prioritizing environmental protection.
- **Quality of products and services:** The code relates to the group's commitment to supplying products and services that adhere to world-class quality standards.
- **Corporate citizenship:** It outlines the group's commitment to good corporate citizenship, including respect for human rights and contribution to community development.
- **Cooperation of Tata Companies:** The code encourages cooperation among Tata companies while respecting the regulatory framework under which they operate.
- **Public representation of the company and the Group:** It provides guidelines for public representation of Tata companies and the Group, stressing on accuracy and consistency in all communications.
- **Third-party representation:** The code outlines principles for dealing with third parties who represent

Tata companies, ensuring they adhere to the same ethical standards.

- **Use of the Tata brand:** It provides guidelines for the use of the Tata brand, underlining the responsibility that comes with using the Tata name.
- **Group policies:** The code references various group policies that provide more detailed guidance on specific areas of conduct.

Now, some key aspects of how the code's group-wide implementation is achieved:

- **Leadership commitment:** The implementation of the code starts at the top, and the code necessitates that leaders across the Tata Group demonstrate their commitment to the codified principles through their business-related decisions.
- **Employee training:** Regular training programmes are conducted to ensure that all employees understand the code and its application in their day-to-day work.
- **Reporting mechanisms:** It establishes mechanisms for reporting violations, including whistleblower protection, to encourage employees to report unethical practices without fear of retaliation.
- **Regular reviews and updates:** The code is reviewed and updated to ensure it remains relevant and addresses new ethical challenges that may arise with changing times.

- **Integration with business processes:** The principles of the code are integrated into various business processes, including recruitment, performance evaluation and decision-making.

Impact and Recognition

The TCOC has played a significant role in shaping the ethical culture of the Tata Group. It has helped maintain the group's reputation for integrity and ethical business practices. The code has also received recognition from various quarters. For instance, in 2015, the Ethisphere Institute recognized Tata Steel and Tata Power as among the World's Most Ethical Companies. Many Tata companies have received this recognition multiple times.

Ratan Tata's implementation of the Code of Conduct offers several valuable lessons for modern business leaders:

- Tata recognized the need to formalize the group's long-held values and ethical principles. By articulating these in a clear document, he ensured consistency across the diverse Tata companies and provided a tangible guide for employees.

- The TCOC applies to all 7,50,000 Tata employees across various companies and countries. This universal approach demonstrates the importance of maintaining consistent ethical standards in a large organization. The requirement for all employees and directors to sign the TCOC and for CEOs to submit annual compliance reports highlights the importance of personal responsibility and accountability in ethical conduct.

- The code outlines commitments to various stakeholders, including employees, customers, communities and the environment. This comprehensive approach teaches leaders to consider the broader impact of their decisions.

- While maintaining its core principles, the TCOC has been periodically refreshed to remain relevant in changing legal and regulatory landscapes. This teaches leaders the importance of evolving ethical guidelines while preserving fundamental values.

- Ratan Tata's personal involvement in developing and promoting the code underscores the critical role of top leadership in maintaining the ethicality of business practices.

- By implementing the TCOC, Ratan Tata demonstrated how ethical conduct contributes to long-term success and reputation building – a valuable lesson for leaders to include principled considerations in their business plans.

- The code serves as a unifying force across the Tata Group, showing how ethical standards can be used to build a strong corporate culture that employees happily adhere to.

- The TCOC's emphasis on fairness, honesty and transparency teaches leaders the value of building trust with all stakeholders.

The Tata Toolkit: Lessons for the Modern Era

Ratan Tata will always be remembered and cherished for the enormous impact he had on the business world. Throughout his career, Tata exemplified the idea that true leadership goes beyond profit margins and shareholder value – that it also encompasses a broader responsibility towards employees, communities and future generations. His approach has inspired countless individuals, both within and outside India, to rethink their perspectives on business and its role in society. These reflections and lessons drawn from his life and work serve as guiding principles for aspiring leaders and established professionals.

Embracing Failure

Ratan's inception of the Tata Nano serves as a powerful reminder that failure is often a stepping stone to success. Despite the Nano's commercial struggles, Tata refused to accept it as a setback and viewed the project as a learning opportunity rather than a defeat. He demonstrated that failures could result in fostering resilience and adaptability, and his experience can help future leaders to embrace failures as part of their journey. Remarking on the commercial failure of the car within a few years of its launch, he said, 'It became termed as the cheapest car by the public and, I am sorry to say, by ourselves, not by me, but the company when it was marketing. I think it was unfortunate.' This perspective encourages individuals to analyse their mistakes critically and use those insights to inform future decisions.

Examining the factors that led to the Nano's failure and the lessons derived from it that can benefit other businessmen, Autocar India editor Hormazd Sorabjee remarked, 'A series of factors has impacted the Nano, right from the Singur issue to cars catching fire to clumsy marketing strategy,' adding, 'There was a bit of overconfidence at the start and not much marketing push from the company. The hype fizzled out even before Tata Motors could effectively roll out sizeable (number of) cars on the road.'

Long-Term Vision

During his leadership of the Tata Group, Ratan Tata demonstrated a remarkable ability to think beyond the present and envision long-term success. When Ratan Tata acquired Jaguar Land Rover (JLR) in 2008, many critics called it a mistake due to the ongoing global financial crisis. However, Tata saw potential where others saw risk. This decision has since paid off handsomely, with JLR becoming a crown jewel in the Tata portfolio and contributing significantly to the group's revenues. His vision for global growth also led to other strategic acquisitions like Tetley Tea and Corus Steel. Furthermore, detecting the potential of the IT industry early on, Ratan Tata invested heavily in building Tata Consultancy Services' capabilities, which ultimately turned from a domestic player into a global IT powerhouse.

Ethical Leadership

Ratan Tata's ethical leadership has been a cornerstone of his legacy that set a benchmark for corporate governance in India and beyond. During the 2008 financial crisis, when many companies sought government bailouts, Tata chose to repay government loans of undisclosed amounts ahead of schedule, a decision that exemplified his moral stance on business practices. Another example of Tata's ethical leadership was evident in his response to the 2008 Mumbai terror attacks. As chairman of

Ratan Tata Quotes

Twenty-five years ago, the launching of the Tata Indica was the birth of India's indigenous passenger car industry. It brings back fond memories and has a special place in my heart for me.

Strive for excellence, but ensure that your efforts benefit those around you.

It's important for the next generation to focus on learning how to think, rather than what to think.

TELCO, long before my time, planted 2,000 trees – it was a terrific thing for a company to do what was not related to its business. Can we create awareness about not polluting our waters? Can we be more sensitive to the environment, not so much by enforcement or by government dictum, but by our own effort? I have been spending a fair amount of time looking at alternate fuels, including hydrogen as a fuel in the future. I headed a government committee to see if it can be a fuel for motorcars in the coming years. Can we look at processes that will be kinder to the environment than we have been, and more sensitive? In fact, I am about to create a cell in Tatas that will look at just that and scan the technologies available that will result in success.

We did a lot things; but trying to reduce the diversity of the group to a fewer number of companies, fewer number of businesses, which is what we set out to do, is something we did not achieve. One of the reasons why we did not achieve that had to do with me.

I don't believe in work-life balance. I believe in work-life integration. Make your work and life meaningful and fulfilling, and they will complement each other.

Ratan Tata Quotes

Success is not measured by what you achieve, but by the opposition you have encountered, and the courage with which you have maintained the struggle against overwhelming odds.

Retirement isn't about playing golf or lying on a beach, reading, whilst sipping on a cocktail. In fact, never before has the urge to do more, been greater.

the Tata Group, he personally went to the affected Taj Hotel site to oversee the rescue operations and show solidarity with employees and guests trapped inside.

This commitment to ethics was further evident in his approach to expansion and acquisitions. When growing the Tata Group from a $5 billion company to a $100 billion enterprise, Ratan Tata was vocal about his refusal to engage in corrupt practices, even in environments where such challenges were prevalent.

Calculated Risk-Taking

Ratan Tata made several business decisions during his career that involved taking calculated risks. He believed in assessing potential outcomes before making daring moves. For example, one of his boldest moves was the acquisition of JLR despite the ongoing worldwide economic crisis. The development of the Tata Nano, marketed as the world's cheapest car, was another calculated risk, although it did not achieve the commercial success initially anticipated. Under Ratan Tata's leadership, the group expanded into various sectors despite criticism for several decisions, allowing the company to weather economic downturns by relying on multiple revenue streams.

Innovation and Adaptation

Ratan Tata's relentless pursuit of innovation and adaptability has been crucial in the Tata Group's success. A noteworthy example is his approach to healthcare. The Cancer Care Programme spearheaded by the Tata Trusts has been providing state-of-the-art cancer treatment facilities across India at lower costs for the underprivileged. Embracing healthcare technology, Tata partnered with organizations to develop telemedicine facilities and digital healthcare platforms for patients in remote locations. Similarly, the Tata Swach by Tata Chemicals – an affordable water purifier designed to provide clean drinking water to millions – is a lesson in responding to critical social needs for business leaders.

Resilience in Adversity

Apart from how Ratan Tata handled the situation, the company faced significant challenges, including a major strike at the plant that turned violent. Another example of his resilience in adversity would be his response to criticism early in his tenure as the chairman of the Tata Group. Many questioned J.R.D. Tata's decision to appoint him, with media branding him as the 'wrong choice'. However, Ratan Tata maintained a dignified silence and focused on proving himself through hard work and dedication, something that he was able to accomplish over the subsequent years. His journey from being doubted to leading the group to unprecedented success demonstrates that resilience, combined with a clear vision and unwavering determination, can overcome initial setbacks and lead to extraordinary achievements.

Focus on Employee Well-Being

Ratan Tata's leadership at the Tata Group exemplifies a profound commitment to employee well-being, offering valuable lessons for modern businessmen and entrepreneurs. During a financial crisis at Tata Steel in 1991, instead of opting for mass lay-offs, Ratan Tata implemented an employee separation scheme (ESS) and a voluntary retirement scheme (VRS). These programmes ensured that employees received full remuneration until their retirement date, along with perennial medical insurance for them and their families. Moreover, over the course of his career he introduced comprehensive corporate wellness programmes with a focus on both physical and mental health and the role they play in workplace productivity. The Tata Group became a pioneer in implementing family-friendly policies and flexible work arrangements. During the 2008 Mumbai terror attacks, Ratan Tata established the Tata Public Service Welfare Trust to provide psychological care and rehabilitation for victims and their families, many of whom struggled with post-traumatic stress disorder (PTSD). This compassionate approach to employee mental health set a new standard for corporate responsibility.

Lifelong Learning

Ratan Tata's unwavering commitment to lifelong learning serves as an inspiring example for students and professionals alike. Throughout his career, he stressed that education extends far beyond obtaining a degree, advocating for the cultivation of a perpetually curious mind. He once remarked, 'Your real learning starts now as you go into the real world. The tools have been given to you, but what you make in life is what you do after you graduate.' This philosophy underscores the importance of continuous growth and adaptation in an ever-changing world. Tata's own journey exemplifies this principle as he pursued architectural studies at Cornell University and graduated with a bachelor's degree in 1962 and later honed his business acumen

On 27 January 2022, Air India officially returned to the Tata Group after 69 years of government ownership, marking a historic moment for both the airline and the conglomerate. This milestone was the culmination of a long and complex process that began with the Indian government's decision to privatize the struggling national carrier. The journey to re-privatization started in earnest in 2017 when the government announced plans to divest its stake in Air India. After initial attempts failed to attract bidders, the government revised its terms, leading to renewed interest. In October 2021, the Tata Group emerged as the successful bidder, offering ₹18,000 crore (approximately $2.4 billion) to acquire the airline. The deal included the purchase of Air India, its low-cost subsidiary Air India Express and a 50 per cent stake in ground handling company AISATS (Air India SATS Airport Services Private Limited). Tata agreed to take on ₹15,300 crore of Air India's debt, with the remaining debt transferred to a government-held company. For Ratan Tata and the Tata Group, this acquisition held deep sentimental value. Air India was founded as Tata Airlines by J.R.D. Tata in 1932, and its return to the fold was seen as a homecoming. Ratan Tata's sentiments about the acquisition were well-known and in line with the group's historical connection to the airline. The acquirement significantly strengthened Tata's position in the Indian aviation sector. It provided access to valuable assets, including over a hundred aircraft, thousands of trained staff and crucial landing slots at airports worldwide. The return of Air India to the Tata Group represented a full-circle moment for the Group and offered hope for the revival of the once-prestigious national carrier under private management.

by completing the Advanced Management Program at Harvard Business School in 1975.

Humility in Leadership

Despite his immense success, Ratan Tata remained humble and approachable, often engaging directly with employees at all levels. The way he used to lead illustrates that true leadership is personified by humility and empathy rather than arrogance or detachment. This lesson encourages leaders to foster an inclusive culture where every voice is valued, promoting collaboration and trust within organizations.

Philanthropy as Purpose

Tata's commitment to philanthropy through the Tata Trusts highlights the significance of giving back to society. He believed businesses should serve a greater purpose beyond profit-making, advocating for corporate social responsibility as integral to business strategy. This perspective teaches future leaders that aligning business goals with social impact can enhance brand reputation while contributing positively to communities.

Navigating Change

Ratan Tata adeptly navigated significant changes within the Indian economy during his tenure as chairman by adapting his strategies according to the evolving market dynamics. His ability to pivot demonstrates the importance of flexibility in leadership – an essential trait for thriving amidst uncertainty.

Building Trust through Transparency

Ratan Tata emphasized transparency in all dealings, believing it fosters trust among stakeholders, employees and consumers. He was a champion for establishing open-door communication channels and feedback mechanisms and encouraged employees at all levels to voice their concerns and ideas freely. Nonetheless, in a 2012 interview, he expressed regret at not having been able to create a 'truly open, flat, transparent organisation' to the extent he had hoped. This candid admission itself demonstrated his commitment to honesty, even when acknowledging shortcomings. Despite this, Ratan Tata's efforts significantly influenced corporate governance in India, with many of the group's practices serving as benchmarks for other companies.

Lessons from Failed Businesses

The Corus Steel Lesson: In 2007, Tata Steel's acquisition of Corus Steel for $12.9 billion was initially hailed as a triumph of Indian industry on the global stage. However, this ambitious move later revealed the perils of overreaching in pursuit of rapid expansion. Former Tata Steel managing director J.J. Irani aptly termed it an 'aspirational mistake', highlighting the risks of such bold ventures. The acquisition, made at the peak of the market, faced significant challenges when the global financial crisis hit shortly after. This experience taught Tata and his team the value of cautious optimism in global expansion strategies and the need to consider potential economic downturns in long-term planning.

The DoCoMo Challenge: The Tata Group's venture into the telecom sector, particularly its partnership with Japanese giant NTT DoCoMo, presented a complex set of challenges that tested Ratan Tata's business acumen. This joint venture was initiated with high hopes but encountered significant hurdles due to regulatory issues and market dynamics. A confluence of factors led to the withdrawal of DoCoMo's partnership with Tata. The venture incurred substantial financial losses of $1.3 billion by April 2014. Tata Teleservices failed to meet agreed-upon performance targets, triggering an exit clause in their agreement. The Indian telecom market also proved challenging, with delayed 3G network roll-outs and regulatory issues. The situation was worsened due to intense competition from new entrants. Ultimately, the combination of financial strain, unmet targets and market challenges led DoCoMo to exercise its contractual right to exit the partnership. The DoCoMo episode taught Tata the importance of anticipating potential regulatory changes and their impact on international agreements. This experience has since informed the Tata Group's approach to international partnerships.

The Ginger Hotels Experience: The Ginger Hotels initiative, launched under Ratan Tata's leadership, aimed to revolutionize the budget hotel segment in India. The hotel chain did achieve some initial success, with forty-two operational properties and over 3,700 rooms by 2018. However, the original vision of rapidly expanding the hotel chain did not materialize as planned. The concept, while innovative, faced challenges in scaling up and meeting diverse market demands across different regions of India. This experience taught Tata the value of continuous market assessment and the need for agility in business models and that even well-conceived ideas require constant refinement and adaptation to succeed in dynamic markets.

Cultural Sensitivity

Ratan Tata's leadership of the Tata Group exemplified a deep understanding of cultural sensitivity in global business operations. As the conglomerate expanded its footprint to over eighty countries, he placed importance on respecting and adapting to local customs and practices. For example, despite taking control of the iconic British brand JLR, Ratan Tata ensured that their heritage and local craftsmanship were preserved and honoured. He maintained the existing management structure and manufacturing facilities in the UK, demonstrating respect for the local workforce.

Importance of Mentorship

Ratan Tata valued mentorship and often took time to guide young entrepreneurs within his organization or through various initiatives aimed at fostering new talent. His belief in nurturing future leaders emphasizes the significance of mentorship in developing skills and confidence among emerging professionals, making it a critical investment for any organization's future.

Emphasis on Teamwork

Ratan Tata's emphasis on teamwork was a cornerstone of his leadership philosophy. Throughout his tenure at the Tata Group, he consistently encouraged a culture of collaboration and mutual support. He once said, 'If you want to walk fast, walk alone. But if you want to walk far, walk together.' He also implemented collaborative decision-making processes that encouraged ideas from employees at every level, believing that diverse perspectives lead to better outcomes. This inclusive approach is reflected in his quote, 'The best leaders are those most interested in surrounding themselves with assistants and associates smarter than they are.'

Setting High Standards

Ratan Tata was dedicated to setting high standards in both quality and ethical practices, which is exemplified in the Tata Code of Conduct – the group's core values and ideals. His insistence on integrity is reflected in the code's first core value, 'We will be fair, honest, transparent and ethical in our conduct; everything we do must stand the test of public scrutiny.' This principle was demonstrated in practice when Ratan Tata refused to engage in unethical practices during the 2G spectrum scam in India despite potential financial losses.

Balancing Profit with Purpose

Ratan Tata's leadership at the Tata Group exemplified a remarkable balance between profit and purpose, demonstrating that business success and social responsibility are not mutually exclusive. Under his guidance, the Tata Group consistently allocated a significant portion of its profits to philanthropic causes. Through the Tata Trusts, over 60 per cent of the group's profits were directed towards education, healthcare and rural development initiatives. Additionally, when Tata Chemicals introduced Tata Salt in 1983, it was not just a business venture but also a solution to the public health concerns raised by iodine and iron deficiencies in the population. Similarly, the development of the Tata Nano had aimed to make transportation accessible to the masses.

Ratan Tata Quotes

- What really motivated me, and sparked a desire to produce such a vehicle, was constantly seeing Indian families on scooters, maybe the child sandwiched between the mother and father, riding to wherever they were going, often on slippery roads. One of the benefits of being in the School of Architecture, it had taught me to doodle when I was free. At first we were trying to figure out how to make two wheelers safer, the doodles became four wheels, no windows, no doors, just a basic dune buggy. But I finally decided it should be a car. The Nano, was always meant for all our people.

- In a world where brand strength is the key to success, the acquisition of the Tetley brand will provide Tata Tea a valuable global opportunity.

- It became termed as the cheapest car by the public and, I am sorry to say, by ourselves, not by me, but the company when it was marketing. I think it was unfortunate.

- Be persistent and resilient in the face of challenges, for they are the building blocks of success.

- It's the largest acquisition by an Indian company abroad. As the country is opening up, it is significant that Tata Tea is going international, acquiring companies and reputed brands abroad.

- What I would like to do is to leave behind a sustainable entity of a set of companies that operate in an exemplary manner in terms of ethics, values and continue what our ancestors left behind.

Ratan Tata Quotes

- My father wanted me to become an engineer; so I spent two years at Cornell as an engineering student, didn't like it and switched to architecture – which is what I wanted to do – and graduated as an architect. I went on to complete structural engineering, which was more to my liking and interest, rather than mechanical engineering, and graduated. I had a very happy time at Cornell; the five-year course for the architecture degree, along with the two-year structural engineering programme, made it seven years. Mainly because architecture design is a five-year degree course and you cannot get a credit for anything, you have to go through the full five years.

- I have always been very confident and very upbeat about the future potential of India. I think it is a great country with great potential.

- The biggest risk is not taking any risk. In a world that is changing quickly, the only strategy that is guaranteed to fail is not taking risks.

- The best leaders are those most interested in surrounding themselves with assistants and associates smarter than they are.

- [Telco was] the first company in which I could actually do something. In other companies, I was always put in a fire-fighting situation.

- My first directorship was that of Nelco and the status of that company has forever been held against me. No one wanted to see that Nelco did become profitable, that it went from a 2% market share to a 25% market share.

Ratan Tata Quotes

- After TCS, I was made the director-in-charge of Nelco (The National Radio & Electronics Company) which, at that time, was losing a large amount of money. For some reason, Nelco, in perception terms, is something that is held against me. Actually, it was a great success story because during my time with Nelco, we moved the market share of radios from 2% to 20%. We wiped out the losses and paid dividends. The only thing that we didn't do (which is because we did not get any infusion of cash from the Tatas) is that we didn't really grow. The consumer electronics business needed a lot of cash to grow.

- We were too conservative about the liberalisation but tried to change when market was opened in 1991... We, however, did better compared to other companies in the open market.

- The cultural tone of the organisation has to be set by the person at the top ... His life, his integrity, his values are those that he can impose on others if he follows them himself.

- You need to go home at night and say, I didn't succumb.

- Be driven by a desire to make a difference, a desire to be ethical and fair. And then you will make a difference.

- Do what you believe is right and do what you believe is fair and do what you believe is going to make a difference.

- Taking decisions is a very lonely activity. Difficult decisions are really ones that you need to take and you're alone.

Ratan Tata Quotes

- None can destroy iron, but its own rust can. Likewise, none can destroy a person, but their own mindset can.

- Never underestimate the power of kindness, empathy, and compassion in your interactions with others.

- There are many times that I feel lonely about not having a wife or a family, and sometimes I long for it. Sometimes I enjoy the freedom of not having to worry about the feelings of someone else or the concerns of someone else. On other times, it does get a little lonely.

- It was in LA that I fell in love and almost got married. But at the same time, I had made the decision to move back, at least temporarily, since I had been away from my grandmother, who wasn't keeping too well, for almost seven years. So I came back to visit her and thought that the person I wanted to marry would come to India with me, but because of the 1962 Indo-China war, her parents weren't okay with her making the move anymore, and the relationship fell apart.

- Now that the monsoons are here, a lot of stray cats and dogs take shelter under our cars. It is important to check under our car before we turn it on and accelerate to avoid injuries to stray animals taking shelter. They can be seriously injured, handicapped and even killed if we are unaware of their presence under our vehicles. It would be heartwarming if we could all offer them temporary shelter when it is pouring this season.

- There has been more time to be at home, play with my dogs, and catch upon smaller things which I never found the time to do earlier.

Ratan Tata Quotes

- From affordable cancer treatment to looking into making the lives in rural India easier – I'm looking forward to this chapter of making it happen at the Tata Trusts.

- No more looking at newspapers and worrying about the bad stuff ... retirement isn't about playing golf, or lying on a beach, reading whilst sipping on a cocktail. In fact, never before has the urge to do more, been greater.

- I would say that one of the things I wish I could do differently would be to be more outgoing.

- Integrity, consistency, and purpose must be the driving forces of any successful business.

- If you were to challenge me, I would say that there may be areas that one may want to enter – like nuclear power, or retailing or real estate or whatever, wherever there are opportunities – even alternate fuels, because it reduces our dependence on fossil fuels. But all of those, in a manner of speaking, are mundane extensions of existing businesses. Today, I think some of us, like Mukesh Ambani, myself and those of us who head industrial units, ought to really focus on what we can really do to make the world a safer place, maybe fifty or one hundred years from now.

www.ingramcontent.com/pod-product-compliance
Lightning Source LLC
LaVergne TN
LVHW010615100826
845148LV00014B/2973

* 9 7 8 9 3 5 7 3 1 8 5 0 1 *